Violin Virtuosos

STRING LETTER PUBLISHING

Publisher: David A. Lusterman
Editors: Mary VanClay and Stacey Lynn
Associate Editor: Jessamyn Reeves-Brown
Assistant Editor: Marsha Gonick
Production Director: Ellen Richman
Designer: Ray Larsen
Production Artist: Susan Pinkerton
Production Coordinator: Judy Zimola
Marketing Manager: Jennifer Fujimoto

Contributors: Edith Eisler, Robert Moon, Andrew Palmer, Timothy Pfaff, Russell
Platt, Julia Zaustinsky
Contents © 2000 by String Letter Publishing, Inc.
David A. Lusterman, Publisher
ISBN 1-890490-31-8

Front cover: Joshua Bell, photograph by Mark Sink.
Back cover: Joshua Bell, photograph by Walter H. Scott; Leila Josefowicz, photo-
graph by Suzie Maeder; Kyung-Wha Chung, photograph courtesy Columbia Artists
Management.

Printed in the United States of America.
PO Box 767, San Anselmo, California 94979
(415) 485-6946; www.stringsmagazine.com

Library of Congress Cataloging-in-Publication Data

Violin virtuosos.
        p. cm. -- (Strings backstage)
    ISBN 1-890490-31-8
    1. Violinists–Interviews. I. Strings (San Anselmo, Calif.) II. Series.

ML 398 .V56 2000
787.2'092'2–dc21
[B]
                                                              00-058820

STRING LETTER PUBLISHING

CONTENTS

INTRODUCTION

Lovers of the violin could hardly be living in a more stimulating era. The interested listener can easily find recordings of great players of the past. Meanwhile, the number of current violinists worthy of the term *virtuoso* is nothing short of remarkable. Talented players from around the world are taking to the concert stage, and through them today's audiences are enjoying the beauty of contemporary composition while falling in love again with traditional works.

In this book, *Strings'* second collection of profiles of active violinists, we explore the many paths of the virtuoso. What is it like to be a superstar soloist? The players acknowledge there are ups and downs. Vadim Repin admits, "Of course one gets tired [of traveling]. Everything you do has its good and its negative side." But when Joshua Bell states, "I love performing more than anything else," we glimpse the impulse that keeps these players going during dozens and even hundreds of concerts every year.

There is much more to the art of fine playing than commanding center stage. Nearly every player claims a deep love of that most intimate form of expression, chamber music. As Leila Josefowicz puts it, "Chamber music is essential. It varies a career, and fortifies it. And there's nothing more thrilling than really hitting it off with one of your colleagues."

Then there are those players who receive less media attention but just as much admiration from colleagues and true music lovers: the concertmasters. We hear from Joseph Silverstein, whose career has spanned close to five decades, much of it as leader of the Boston Symphony Orchestra and the Utah Symphony. He has played under some of the century's finest conductors (and conducts himself), and he speaks of the "wonderful, quick seduction" that goes on between guest conductor and orchestra, as well as the deeper relationships forged over the years between section leader and section, director and orchestra. Jorja Fleezanis, leader of the Minnesota Orchestra for nearly a dozen years, speaks astutely on the topic of playing from within a group versus standing on stage as the soloist. "It's not 'discount' music making," she says. "If anything, it's even more challenging to play those phrases and cadences in an orchestra, in one breath. The collectiveness is what makes the orchestra a powerful place to express yourself."

Many other themes emerge: love of Bach, love of golf, the love *and* fear aroused by the Beethoven Violin Concerto, the excitement of contemporary music, the trials of trying to commit interpretations to record. The similarities and differences among the viewpoints of the 11 players profiled in this book underscore what makes music universal: it allows for endless individual expression, but its passion and beauty speak to us all.

Mary VanClay
Editor

Joshua Bell

American violinist Joshua Bell, still in his early thirties, ranks among the top violinists currently performing. With an established career as orchestral soloist, chamber musician, and recitalist, Bell now also oversees his own annual chamber-music winter festival at London's prestigious Wigmore Hall. He has definitively broken away from the "brat pack" with which he was associated when the following interview first appeared in Strings in 1995.

At that time Bell was just beginning his foray into new music, the genre he's most closely associated with now. He has premiered and recorded works by Aaron Jay Kernis (Air), Nicholas Maw (whose Violin Concerto was not just written for Bell but inspired by him), John Williams' "Porgy and Bess Fantasy" as well as Williams' arrangements of some of the major Gershwin songs, and John Corigliano's soundtrack for the movie The Red Violin, whose central themes Corigliano recomposed into The Red Violin Chaconne. He has also switched record labels from Decca to Sony.

While Bell maintains the standard-issue superstar schedule, a new sense of relaxation has come into his playing. The part of this one-of-a-kind artist that would rather be golfing has also found an outlet in numerous collaborations with bassist Edgar Meyer, multi-instrumentalist Mike Marshall, and others in impressive and popular bluegrass- and country-inspired recordings. It's hard to tell where this tireless young artist will go next. The only sure thing is that the trip won't be boring.

Hanging on Every Note

Timothy Pfaff

Photo by Mark Sink

When you're 27 and on your second Strad, you're either from old money or uncommonly gifted. Joshua Bell, the son of an Indiana University psychology professor, is paying for his "Tom Taylor" Antonio Stradivari violin with one of the more arresting talents to have emerged from the American heartland in recent memory. Just old enough to have played with Rudolf Serkin at Marlboro, and young enough to have to work at carving out his own niche in the young-violinists' brat pack, Bell has proved adroit at traveling lightly between the old and new worlds, the "Tom Taylor" snuggling with his Power Mac.

Growing up in Bloomington not only landed Bell in the front yard of one of America's great music schools; it also made him a virtual neighbor of one of the world's great violin teachers, the late Josef Gingold, with whom he studied for a decade. Since then, the open-faced, open-voweled, middle-American whiz kid has earned the respect of audiences and his fellow musicians throughout the world. His disarming personal honesty and the utter lack of evidence that there has ever been a silver spoon in his mouth have hastened a judgmental world's willingness to forgive Bell for simultaneously looking good in the infamous stone-washed jeans and doing things his own, rather oddly old-fashioned way. It's easy to pardon someone for a rapidly growing London/Decca discography at an indecently early age when said recording artist weighs in as an unabashed fan of consonant tonality.

Identifying traits of Bell's playing are a honeyed yet not overly viscous tone, an uncompromised beauty of sound that doesn't favor tone quality over musical rhetoric, a keen attention to local detail within a firm sense of overall musical architecture, and an inclination toward spontaneity and even risk-taking without a trace of personal or artistic recklessness. A predilection for sports is reflected in a platform manner that is energized but highly disciplined, tightly coiled, and, in moments of extreme absorption, introverted, even diffident in appearance. Although he has consolidated a reputation as a concerto soloist in demand by the world's best orchestras and conductors, Bell is as well known as an accomplished chamber musician.

Strings caught up with Bell in January [1995] when he was appearing with the Seattle Symphony, playing the Lalo *Sinfonie Espagnole*, which he was also about to take on a European tour with Charles Dutoit conducting the Orchestre National de France. Alert and well rested, Bell proved a thoughtful, engaging, and forthcoming conversationalist, holding his own in a way that only an experienced soloist with a sure sense of himself could manage.

It feels momentous that our interview has fallen mere weeks after the death of your great teacher, Josef Gingold. What has that been like for you?

It's very sad, and it really hasn't quite hit me yet. I can't quite believe that he's not still around anymore. Just the other day I listened to his recording of Kreisler, which I still think is maybe the best Kreisler recording there is.

I had been trying to prepare myself for it. He was old, and he had health problems. But I just spent New Year's Day with him, and he was in the best mental state I'd seen him in for years. We spent the whole afternoon together and talked about everything under the sun. He gave me advice and music and an autographed picture of himself that I'd been meaning to ask him for. It was the last time I saw him. I feel really wonderful to have had that time. There was a sense of closure to it. The very next day he had the heart attack and was in the hospital.

I had studied with him for ten years, from when I was 12 to when I was 22. He was my mentor, my grandfather, almost. There is no one to take his place, and I'm past the point of trying to find a mentor like that. He always had advice, often repertoire advice. He'd come up with something I wouldn't have thought of, because he was an encyclopedia. He was known for that.

For me he was the best kind of teacher. He was able to play, to demonstrate, which I think is the greatest asset a teacher can have. He wasn't the kind of teacher who had set fingerings and bowings, like many do. His attitude was that everyone's hand, everyone's technique, is a little bit different—and that the reason for particular fingerings is to serve the music. Having everyone play the same fingerings is the first step to having everyone play the same way. It's how one chooses to play on a string, with what fingering, that makes an interpretation. It was important for me not to be forced into playing a particular way. For some people he wouldn't have been the ideal teacher, because he was very free. But he was just what I needed, and I was very lucky to grow up in Bloomington, around him.

Walter H. Scott

With an established career as orchestral soloist, Bell now also oversees his own annual chamber-music festival at Wigmore Hall.

What would you identify as his legacy in your playing?

Something I will always have in my head is his sound. He strove for a beauty of sound that I think got in my ear. It's that French-Belgian sound, which he got from his teacher, [Eugène] Ysaÿe. That sound is incredibly sweet, almost sugary. I also picked up his sense of intimacy with the music—drawing the audience in instead of belting out to the audience. I hope I play that way, trying to find 20 different colors of pianissimo. That's something that makes an audience listen. He encouraged lots of different bow speeds to create a big palette of colors. And one of the things I work on today is actually getting more of the sound I always resisted, playing very near the bridge. It's the sound that's often taught, big, as big as possible. That's something I didn't like, but now I find it's an important color to have in the palette. That's one of the reasons I feel I'm a Strad player, as [Gingold] was.

There's also an approach to music, especially some of the more Romantic repertoire, that he had, and that someone like Kreisler would represent, that I feel I picked up from him—a sense of rubato, of taking time, which is very difficult to teach: taking time but not losing time. Kreisler would sound incredibly free, but his rhythm was spot-on. And I learned from Gingold that there should always be a long line—

What He Plays

Joshua Bell owns and plays the "Tom Taylor" Antonio Stradivari (strung with Thomastik Dominant strings), which he bought in 1994. Made in Cremona in 1732, it is Bell's second Stradivari, succeeding the cut-down, guitar-shaped 1726 instrument he had bought from a Chicago violin shop and sold to acquire the "Tom Taylor."

Bell first tried out the "Tom Taylor" in the Chicago shop of Bein and Fushi. "Then I had to leave town," he recalls. "I later learned they had sold it to someone in the Stradivari Society, a consortium of musical-instrument buyers, wealthy people who buy instruments and lend them to young people who need them. Bein and Fushi called to tell me they had sold the instrument and to ask if I wanted to play it. I played on it for a couple of years, eventually buying it myself.

"That's the ideal way to buy an instrument. Because violins are so valuable, dealers can't let you try them for more than a few days. I was considering the 'Tom Taylor,' but before I plunked down my life's earnings, I wanted to make sure I had the right one. I had tried many Strads, and a few del Gesùs, and I once fell in love with a Guarneri from a shop in Europe. I almost made an offer on it, but I decided to take it out for a week. After a week, I didn't want to hear another note out of that instrument, which had a very one-dimensional sound. Buying it right away would have been like marrying someone after the first date. The 'Tom Taylor' stood the test of time. I realized that the instrument I lived with for two years and loved was the one I wanted to have."

Bell appreciates the fact that the "Tom Taylor" is well documented, "almost back to when it was made. At one time it was in the collection of [Nicolò] Paganini, and later in the [19th] century Joseph Joachim had it. So it's had a good history. "It's a real player's instrument. Some violins are in pristine condition but have not been played; they seem more like museum pieces. This one is in good, not perfect, shape—it's got some patches underneath—but it should be played, not kept behind glass. It has all its original parts, except for the neck, which was extended, probably in the 19th century. And it has much of the original varnish.

"I basically use one bow, a Tourte that used to belong to Samuel Dushkin. He was a friend of Stravinsky and transcribed a lot of Stravinsky's music for the violin. A couple of violins also have his name. Pinchas Zukerman plays the Dushkin Guarneri, for example. My teacher, Josef Gingold, also played on a Strad and a Tourte.

"For a Tourte it's on the stiffer side; usually they're fairly soft. They make a beautiful sound, but sometimes they're hard to manage because they are so soft. On my instrument, this bow creates a round, warm sound. There are times when I wish it had more bite and edge, but I love this darker, rounder sound. I may be foolish—Tourtes are so valuable—but I use it all the time."

that the violin is a very vocal instrument. Sometimes the way one would sing something is the most natural way to play it.

The "anything goes" philosophy I see so much of today is disturbing to me, because so much about music is rules. Form is very important. Interpretation is like architecture: you can have all these great ideas, but the problem in the end is how to make the building stand up.

You have an avowed interest in historical violinists. Sometimes I hear in your playing a comparable kind of freedom with the music.

They were the ones I was exposed to early, and Gingold comes from that tradition. A mistake kids make today is trying to copy those players. There was a whole school of Heifetz copiers for a while. But you can't copy anything and have it seem interesting. You can tell when something comes directly from the heart.

What is involved in making a piece your own?

Being completely convinced by a piece. When I'm playing a Beethoven sonata, I really am trying to get into what Beethoven wanted—but I'm the one deciding what I think Beethoven wanted. In the process, I become convinced that this is the way it should be.

You have to make it as if you are writing it, as though it is something new, being written right there on the spot. You can't go on autopilot and then come to life when you suddenly connect with a note or phrase. Every single note has a direction, either coming somewhere or going somewhere. Until you feel that, you probably shouldn't play a piece.

When someone hears me playing, I don't particularly want people to think, "I'm listening to Joshua Bell." I want them to go away thinking, "God, that's a great piece."

A lot of the repertoire you play is familiar music. How do you make it your own without distorting it?

To start with, one has to look at the composer's instructions. As simple as that sounds, it's amazing how rarely people do that. The composer writes instructions about his musical approach to the piece, and 99 percent of the time what the composer writes as far as dynamics and tempo markings is the best way to play the piece.

What the composer wrote can be overruled, but only after extreme consideration. It's always a difficult decision. I've done it with the Schumann Violin Concerto, which I've just recorded with the Cleveland Orchestra under Christoph von Dohnányi. The piece is very, very late, and Schumann wrote it very quickly. It was never revised the way Brahms' concerto was, by Joachim. It has some of the most amazing stuff—but I had to change a lot of things, including some notes. The piece is quirky, but I never saw Schumann's music as being insane. It's far out, but not insane. The slow movement is one of the most beautiful slow movements; it's very subtle. Schumann is one of my favorite composers. His music is very intimate. It's hard to make work, and it's musically very difficult, but that doesn't make it any less great than Brahms.

Do you feel any gravitation toward pre-Classical music?

To Bach, always. He's the ultimate challenge, with the solo sonatas. It's the greatest music. I rarely get a chance to perform those pieces, because I'm usually playing with a pianist. And these days you're so often criticized if you're not playing on original instruments. There are some things about playing it on the modern instrument that are difficult. The four-note chords, for example, would be easier on an earlier instrument. But Bach is the only composer I find interesting pre-Haydn and Mozart. Of course I play [Vivaldi's] *Four Seasons* sometimes.

Mark Sink

I know you have your reservations about the early-music "movement." Are there things you have gotten from musicians of that persuasion?

I've worked with [conductor] Roger Norrington a lot. I like him because he really is a performance man. What I don't like music to become is a museum-type thing. Music comes alive when Roger leads it. And I've learned a lot from the cellist Steven Isserlis. He's a great musician who is interested in early music. He's played things using original setups, and he plays on all gut strings. And I've done the Brahms Double Concerto with Steven and John Eliot Gardiner.

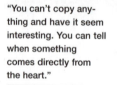

"You can't copy anything and have it seem interesting. You can tell when something comes directly from the heart."

One of the main things I've gotten from that crowd has to do with the use of vibrato. When we're little, we're taught to play with continuous vibrato, which I've learned is not always the best idea. Certainly in the 19th century, vibrato was used as an embellishment, to intensify notes and certain other things. Once you can make a pure sound, almost without vibrato, then you can vary it. Every note should have a different amount of vibrato. It should be that flexible. Instead it often sounds painted on, as if you either have it or you don't. It's important to hear the core of the sound. I want to hear the note.

What's your feeling—and practice—as regards cadenzas? I understand your forthcoming recording of the Brahms [recorded after this interview appeared in 1995] *includes your own cadenza.*

I'm pretty much happy with the way it is—after years of revising it. Now I'm doing all my own cadenzas in the Mozarts, and last summer I was toying with the idea of doing one for the Beethoven. I was playing the Beethoven with André Previn and the Orchestra of St. Luke's, and the day before the concert I started going. I can get really obsessive—I start doing something, and I can't stop. I finished the cadenza just before the concert and decided, 'What the hell, I'm going to play it.' It was scary. It was extremely hard, because I had tried to include too much. That's starting to settle down now. But I love putting my own stamp on concertos. There's no reason everyone shouldn't do it. I'd eventually like to write my own music, period. I'm probably going to try.

Where does that impulse come from?

To write something, even cadenzas, is an incredible feeling, of creating something from nothing. With a cadenza you're borrowing things, but at least it gave me the sense of what it's like to make something up and actually perform it. Everyone used to do that.

Has there been much music written for you?

I've performed four or five pieces. But I've got stacks of music at home that composers have sent me, and I'm so behind as far as getting to look at the pieces because I'm so busy.

The Nicholas Maw concerto is a very good piece. I've played it with Roger [Norrington], and once with Leonard Slatkin. We're probably going to record the piece next summer [see Recordings, page 11]. It's pretty tonal, and harmonically it has meaning for me.

Right now I'm preparing a new piece, *Air,* by Aaron Jay Kernis. It came about from a group of presenters who wanted to commission a piece for me, which had to be by an American composer. I heard some of Kernis' music, and I thought it was neat.

What's performing like for you?

I love performing more than anything else. I feel comfortable on stage. I still get nervous before every performance—not terribly, but I have serious butterflies—and I'm glad. I don't want to lose that. There's stress every time I go out on stage and relief when it's over. But once I start playing, I lose that nervousness. Ideally, when I perform—it doesn't always happen, and it's hard to describe—but when it's perfect, I get into a mental state in which I feel incredibly focused, not thinking about any other distractions, like people in the audience. When it clicks just right, I feel like I can do no wrong. I could change my fingers—do it on a different string—because I have that much concentration. Also, you feel you're inside the music. That only happens under the right circumstances, with an audience that's receptive. In places like Japan, where they're so quiet, sometimes it's almost a weird feeling, because it's hard to feel their participation. Sometimes I don't get the feeling that they're hanging on every note. That's what I like, when people are doing what I'm doing—hanging on every note. It happens when I'm playing with a great pianist or conductor. So it happens maybe five, ten times a year. Chamber music is often the most satisfying. The trio concerts I did last year with Olli Mustonen

Recordings

Aaron Jay Kernis: *Air for Violin; Double Concerto for Violin and Guitar; Lament and Prayer.* With Pamela Frank and Cho-Liang Lin, violin; Sharon Isbin, guitar; Minnesota Orchestra, David Zinman, cond.; St. Paul Chamber Orchestra, Hugh Wolff, cond. (Argo 460226-2).

Barber: *Violin Concerto;* Bloch: *Baal Shem;* Walton: *Violin Concerto.* Baltimore Symphony Orchestra, David Zinman, cond. (London/Decca 452851-2).

Brahms: *Violin Concerto in D, Op. 77;* Schumann: *Violin Concerto in D.* Cleveland Orchestra, Christoph von Dohnányi, cond. (London/Decca 444811-2).

Bruch: *Violin Concerto No. 1 in G, Op. 26;* Mendelssohn: *Violin Concerto in E, Op. 64.* Orchestra of Academy of St. Martin-in-the-Fields, Neville Marriner, cond. (London/Decca 421145-2).

Chausson: *Poeme, Op. 25;* Saint-Saëns: *Introduction et Rondo capriccioso, Op. 28;* Massenet: *"Meditation" from Thais;* Sarasate: *Zigeunerweisen, Op. 20;* Ysaÿe: *Caprice d'apres l'Etude en forme de valse de Saint-Saëns;* Ravel: *Tzigane.* Royal Philharmonic Orchestra, Andrew Litton, cond. (London/Decca 433519-2).

Gershwin Fantasy: *Fantasy for Violin and Orchestra on Porgy and Bess; Three Preludes; Songs for Violin and Orchestra.* With John Williams, piano; London Symphony Orchestra, John Williams, cond. (SK 60659).

The Kreisler Album. Fritz Kreisler: *Praeludium and Allegro; Schön Rosmarin; Tambourin chinois; Caprice viennois; La Precieuse; Liebesfreud; Liebesleid; La gitana; Berceuse romantique; Polichinelle; Rondino; Tempo di minuetto; Toy-Soldiers' March; Allegretto; Marche miniature viennoise; Aucassin and Nicolette; Menuett; Sicilienne and Rigaudon; Syncopation.* With Paul Coker, piano (London/Decca 444409-2).

Listen to the Storyteller: *Three musical tales for children with original scores by Wynton Marsalis, Edgar Meyer, and Patrick Doyle.* With Kate Winslet, Graham Greene, and Wynton Marsalis, narration; Edgar Meyer, bass; Jerry Douglas, Dobro; Orchestra of St. Luke's, Robert Sadin and Steven Mercurio, cond. (SK 60283).

Live from the Spoleto Festival USA, 1986. Kodaly: *Duo, Op. 7;* Mozart: *Quartet in F, K. 370;* Vivaldi: *Concerto in D, RV 95.* With Carter Brey, cello; Douglas Boyd, oboe; Scott Nickrenz, viola; Paula Robison, flute; David Finckel, cello; Kenneth Cooper, harpsichord (MMD 60152W/53M).

Live from the Spoleto Festival USA, 1987. *Brahms: Piano Quartet No. 3. With Scott Nickrenz, viola; Carter Brey, cello; Jeffrey Kahane, piano (MMD 60189T).*

Maw: Violin Concerto. London Philharmonic Orchestra, Sir Roger Norrington, cond. (SK 62856).

Mozart: Violin Adagio, K. 261; Violin Concertos Nos. 3 and 5; Rondo, K. 373. English Chamber Orchestra, Peter Maag, cond. (London 436376).

Presenting Joshua Bell: *Works by Wieniawski, Sibelius, Brahms/Joachim, Paganini, Bloch, Nováček, Schumann/Auer, Falla/Kreisler, Grasse, Sarasate. With Samuel Sanders, piano (London/Decca 417891-2).*

Prokofiev: Violin Concerto No. 1 in D, Op. 19; Violin Concerto No. 2 in G, Op. 63; The Love for Three Oranges. Orchestre Symphonie de Montreal, Charles Dutoit, cond. (London/Decca 440331-2).

Prokofiev: Violin Sonata in F, Op. 80; Five Melodies, Op. 35 bis; Violin Sonata in D Major, Op. 94 bis. With Olli Mustonen, piano (London/Decca 440926-2).

The Red Violin: *Original Motion Picture Soundtrack Composed by John Corigliano. Philharmonia Orchestra, Esa-Pekka Salonen, cond. (SK 63010).*

Saint-Saëns: Violin Concerto No. 3; Lalo: Symphonie Espagnole. Orchestre Symphonique de Montreal, Charles Dutoit, cond. (London/Decca 425501-2).

Short Trip Home: *Music by Edgar Meyer. With Edgar Meyer, bass; Sam Bush and Mike Marshall, mandolin (SK 60864 S1; SSV 5790).*

Shostakovich: Trios Nos. 1 and 2; Messiaen: Quartet for the End of Time. With Steven Isserlis, cello; Olli Mustonen, piano; Michael Collins, clarinet (London/Decca 452899-2).

Sibelius: Violin Concerto, Op. 47. Goldmark: Violin Concerto No. 1. Los Angeles Philharmonic Orchestra, Esa-Pekka Salonen, cond. (SK 65949).

Tchaikovsky: Violin Concerto in D, Op. 35; Wieniawski: Violin Concerto No. 2 in D, Op. 22. Cleveland Orchestra, Vladimir Ashkenazy, cond. (London/Decca 421716-2).

and Steven Isserlis were among my best musical experiences, in terms of pure energy in the air.

You've done a significant amount of work with an interesting group of pianists—like Mustonen.

He's a monster, and a genius, too. At the Wigmore in London, we're going to be playing a nonette he has composed. I don't know that it's been played before. Olli really owns the music when he plays it, often to a point that disturbs people. He's so personal. I would travel distances to hear him play pretty much anything. There's always logic to everything he does.

There have been times when Olli and I have not been able to agree. Last year we programmed the Kreutzer Sonata—and when we rehearsed it, we realized that it wasn't going to work. He's not the kind of player who can go halfway. Some pieces you can compromise on, but in this case it was like I'd have to play it like him or he'd have to play it like me, and we realized it wasn't going to work. We just changed the repertoire. It probably saved the friendship, not doing that piece.

How do you characterize yourself as a musician? You seem very rational to me.

Rational is the best compliment you could give me. I like the mathematical aspects of music, too. I like the order. I like things to make sense. And the musicians I most admire don't play purely from the gut.

That everything you do is honest—that's the most important thing in a performance. You're not thinking in terms of the effect it will create. You're exposing yourself and the way you feel. I think an audience picks that up. Sometimes I get discouraged, when I see frauds who are successful.

What about your process? You've talked about leaving your violin alone for days at a time.

I've never been a big practicer, I guess. I go in spurts. Sometimes it's hard to get myself to do the repetition that's necessary. With something like the Mendelssohn Concerto that I know so well, it's hard to do the required practice—which I still need to do.

I have a lot of other interests, and I'm into other things. When I was a kid, say 12 to 16, I was so into video games, I'd often go a week without practicing. Now I wish I had practiced more when I was younger because I would have learned more repertoire. You learn more quickly when you're young.

But I still love music; I don't beat it to death. And I haven't had any physical problems, either. Usually you get tendinitis when you play a lot; it begins to hurt, and you continue playing. If it starts to hurt for me, I just stop and do something else.

I have a lot of habits I'm still breaking from very early childhood, as far as playing. I should mention my teacher before Mr. Gingold, Mimi

Zweig. She's becoming an important teacher for young kids. She has a huge academy in Indiana in the summertime. After my original teacher of four years, she brought me back to basics. She made me go through all the Kreutzer études and things like that—and made me play correctly.

But if I had practiced six hours a day the way I play, I would probably have problems, because I'm not always the most relaxed or efficient. The ideal in that regard is Heifetz, who is my idol. If you watch him play, it's almost eerie. I think that's why people called him cold, because his economy of motion was unbelievable. I try to do as little extra motion as possible. But you have to be careful not to stifle yourself.

What are your other interests?

I've always been interested in sports, mostly tennis and basketball. A big passion of mine is golf, believe it or not. It has applications to so many other things. It's more than a sport—it's almost Zenlike, the focus in every shot. You know exactly what you have to do, and it's just you.

A golf swing looks so simple—and it's so complicated. It's like drawing a sound out of an instrument. It's something pros work on their entire lives. It looks like a pro is doing it slowly without any

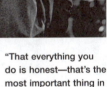

"That everything you do is honest—that's the most important thing in a performance."

effort. You can swing for all you're worth and it won't go ten feet, but if you learn to transfer all your energy in the right direction, you can do it very easily, and the ball will go miles. Sometimes you totally relax and feel like you're hardly swinging, and the ball will go 200 yards. It's the same with the sound when you're playing. You're using your muscles, and when they all work together, rather than against each other, and you can totally relax your arm and use very little effort, you can produce a very big sound. That goes against your initial inclination to press down.

I also still love computer games. There's one I could spend ten hours a day playing called Crystal Caliber. What I like about it is that you're going for a higher score. With other games, you might just want to be completing the game. But I want to beat my own high score. And there's a national registry for the highest scorers of this game. Right now I'm fourth place in the nation—and I'm desperate to beat this No. 1 score, which is by some guy from Eugene, Oregon.

But can he play Lalo?

Good question. I should e-mail him.

Leila Josefowicz

Leila Josefowicz followed the prodigy's path, performing on NBC's television tribute to Bob Hope when she was just ten years old. Half a dozen years later, however, she received national attention when she made her Carnegie Hall debut performing the Tchaikovsky Concerto with Sir Neville Marriner and the Academy of St. Martin in the Fields. Since then her career in both the U.S. and Europe has shot forward; she's appeared with such orchestras as the Boston and Chicago Symphonies, the Los Angeles and London Philharmonics, and the Deutsches-Symphonie-Orchester Berlin, to name a few. She is also active in chamber music, collaborating with violinist and violist Jaime Laredo, pianists Martha Argerich and André Watts, and many others.

Josefowicz is a graduate of the Curtis Institute of Music in Philadelphia and a recipient of the 1994 Avery Fisher Career Grant. She now lives in Florida with her husband, conductor Kristjan Järvi, and their young son, Lukas. In this interview from the spring of 2000, she discusses the ways in which recent changes, both personal and professional, have affected her career and her approach to making music.

Adult Prodigy

Andrew Palmer

Photo by Suzie Maeder

The kid has grown up. Forget the sparky teenager, all teeth and long hair, seen in her early publicity photos. And ignore the more recent image, reproduced on her *For the End of Time* CD, in which a nervous-looking waif, hair pulled back into a spiky ponytail, stares uncertainly at the camera. The 22-year-old woman who walks into the rehearsal hall in Birmingham, England, is most definitely an adult: casually dressed, hair tied back haphazardly, and displaying the unmistakable profile of a mother-to-be. The everyday Leila Josefowicz is, if not unrecognizable from her airbrushed marketing image, a far cry from it.

Fortunately she's as media-friendly as ever and agreed readily to this interview. As I'm about to discover, she talks candidly, expressing opinions that are thoughtful and mature. Yet now that the rehearsal of Bruch's G-Minor Concerto is over, the authority she demonstrated on stage has evaporated, leaving her slightly ill at ease and, from time to time, even a little tongue-tied. We begin by discussing how "normal" a life she's had. This is the woman, don't forget, whose appearance at the age of ten on a Bob Hope TV special, playing Wieniawski's Scherzo-tarantelle, was introduced by Lucille Ball.

"I do realize now how different a life I've led—even to this day—from that of most people my age," she says. "For a while I wasn't sure how to come to grips with it, or whether I truly liked it. And the way I've dealt with it, for the most part, is to not think about it much. Until a few months ago I was playing nonstop—which was a kind of learning experience for me, because after a while I thought, 'Why do this? Why confine yourself so much that you can't enjoy what you're doing?' I've now reached the point where I'm discovering the groove that I want to go in—in my career as well as in other aspects of my life."

It all began in October 1977, when Josefowicz was born in Mississaugga, Ontario, in Canada. Her father, a scientist, has always loved the violin, and when Leila was three years old, he started her on the Suzuki method. At around the same time, the family moved to California, one hour's drive north of Los Angeles. The stage was set, both musically and geographically, for the development of a remarkable talent.

"Although it was a dream of my father's that I should play the violin, my parents had no idea it would ever turn into this," Josefowicz remembers. "After a few years I realized that I actually had a chance of making it professionally. You have to believe that you can have a crack at whatever you want to do, and in this I had incredible support from my family. Some people would have called it pressure, I guess—it depends who you talk to—but without that kind of help I couldn't have succeeded." She cites a clear example: when, at age eight, she had virtually finished with the production-line Suzuki method, her parents found a teacher who was able to encourage her individuality as a performer. He lived several hours' drive away, but twice a week they drove her to and from her lessons.

"I was never in a very strict Suzuki program," she continues, "and that was good, because it can be very 'by the book.' Technically, my playing had never really been by the rules—the way I fingered certain things and the way I sometimes used my bowing arm weren't always in the style they wanted. In those days, of course, I spent most of my time developing technique. But 'technique' is a strange word to use, really, because it means something different to each person. To some people it's dexterity; to others, including me, it's the ability to convey emotionally exactly what you want to. In the end, technical conventions don't really matter as long as you get your point across."

Josefowicz's school life was a mix of the normal and the extraordinary. Her parents negotiated a special arrangement whereby she studied core subjects during what would otherwise have been free periods; in this way she was able to leave school by 1:30 each afternoon and use the precious hour or two thus saved to drive to her violin lesson or to practice at home. "Looking back on those years, the value of one hour a day was amazing!" she recalls. "I wanted to do well at school—to take full advantage of what was being offered to me—and of course I had homework. So there was a huge amount of juggling to do. I must say, I'm glad that part of my life is over."

Suzie Maeder

While her brother, three years her junior, was leading an ordinary, nonmusical life (now 19, he's studying at the University of California at Berkeley), Leila was becoming a child star and joining the local celebrity circuit. "There were a lot of gala evenings in downtown L.A. and Beverly Hills, honoring presidents or stars, and the prodigies used to go along and perform," she explains. "I took part in lots of these galas and got to meet a lot of presidents! I was always the little kid who had to wow everybody, you know? When I was ten, the producer of one of these evenings was put in charge of a TV tribute to Bob Hope, to be broadcast nationwide, and he included me in the show.

"Although it was a dream of my father's that I should play the violin, my parents had no idea it would ever turn into this."

"It was a huge event. Reagan made a speech, as did Bob Hope. Andrew Lloyd Webber made a special appearance, and the Martha Graham Dance Company was there. Even Van Cliburn played in the show. So I was in amazing company and received an enormous amount of media coverage. But I didn't have any idea at the time just what it all meant. It's funny: if I hadn't grown up in Los Angeles, the amount of media attention I got would have been completely different. That is, if I got any at all. In this business, so much can rely on just one event that suddenly changes the scope of things."

It's not to diminish Josefowicz's huge talent to suggest that her early celebrity was founded largely on youth. That, after all, is the basis of a child prodigy's appeal. It's well known, too, that not every child star survives the transition into adulthood, either musically or psychologically. For some young shoulders, the pressures are too great.

"Prodigies grow up with their instruments from such a young age," Josefowicz says, "and they're trained to think only in terms of music. This makes you work very, very hard and maintain the right priorities to achieve your goal of becoming a world-class player. Practicing is, in

What She Plays

The intimacy of a soloist's relationship with her instrument might be hard for some people to understand. "It's very intimate," Josefowicz agrees. "But what's even more intimate is the relationship you have to have with yourself! I mean, in order to play music really comfortably, you have to be ready to take all the risks, emotionally and physically—the instrument being the vehicle."

Turning to the subject of her own violin, she adds, "I don't have a name for him, as some soloists have for their instruments." But it's definitely a "he," then? "Well, tomorrow it might be a 'she,' you know?"

Josefowicz acquired him or her—the "Ebersolt" Giuseppe Guarneri del Gesù of 1739—in what she describes as "one of those amazing moments that you know you'll remember forever." Four years ago she played the Sibelius Concerto at Carnegie Hall with the Boston Symphony and Seiji Ozawa, and after the performance the ichthyologist and instrument collector Herbert Axelrod went backstage to meet her. "He's an amazing person," she remarks. "He just said, 'Well, how would you like to play one of my del Gesùs?' At this point I just gripped something near me so that I wouldn't fall over! Then I said, 'Absolutely. I would love to.' The instrument has been on loan to me since then.

"It's a great violin. Most del Gesùs sound dark, but this particular instrument is even darker. I like its tone very, very much. It's also very responsive. In fact, it has the same playing characteristics of most del Gesùs: the more you put in, the more comes out."

She has four bows and changes between them according to the work she's performing. (Or, she admits, if one of them needs rehairing.) "I have a Persois, which is amazing because it's very light but very strong and makes a great sound. For heavier works I use a Pajeot, and I also have a Tourte—it's not clear whether it's 'school of' or François. I've shown it to many people, and it always arouses curiosity. But everyone tells me something different about it, so I really don't know. I also have a modern bow made by Lee Guthrie [of Hudson, Wisconsin]. It's a great bow—very strong and supple."

Her E string is a Wondertone Stark by Pirastro, which she finds gives a richer sound, and feels less flimsy, than most others. Her A and D strings are Dominants—"they're pretty standard, but more or less foolproof"—and she's been experimenting with different Gs. "The Dominant has always been fine, but I've been looking for even more quality of sound to go with the volume. At the moment I'm trying this new Pirelli G, which I like a lot. This might be it. We'll see!"

fact, not something you must do for a certain amount of hours every day. It's not the same as an athlete's training. But as a young musician who does need to practice every day because you have to develop a certain amount of technique, you're made to believe it is.

"Fortunately, I went to public schools because my parents thought it would be better for my social life. They were absolutely right, though I'm still discovering the whole business of 'personal relations.' It's important for a musician, because you can't rely just on playing; to make music with people, you have to associate with them."

Presumably you also have to know how to communicate your feelings? "Exactly. Music is so human. So the players who can develop relationships with other performers always do better.

"I'd say that only in the last few years have I started to find my 'voice.' Although playing always felt comfortable and natural to me, there's such a difference now in knowing what I want to do musically, and in getting the kind of sounds I've wanted to have. It's amazing to me how few performers exploit the huge range of possible tone colors, speeds of vibrato, and so on. I mean, we all have to produce many different sounds, yet so many players seem to have only one sound."

From age 13 to age 18, Josefowicz studied at the Curtis Institute with Joseph Brodsky and Jaime Laredo, and her parents moved to Philadelphia to be with her. (Her father's employers have also been very supportive of her career and in this instance found a job for him in the local branch of the company.) By the end of this period she had signed with IMG Artists and secured an exclusive recording contract with Philips Classics. She was introduced to the label by conductor Sir Neville Marriner, who had worked with her while directing the Los Angeles Chamber Orchestra. Costa Pilavachi, then head of Philips in Amsterdam [and now president of its parent group, Universal Music], took some colleagues to hear her audition and came away impressed.

"We all know that the music we love is fantastic," he explains, "but you need the right artist, with the right personality, to communicate that to each new generation. Ask a young person today if they've ever heard of Jascha Heifetz and Nathan Milstein, and you'll find they haven't. But they'll discover the great concertos and sonatas through a performer they can identify with. When we heard Leila we felt she was that type of artist."

Her first CD for Philips, the Tchaikovsky and Sibelius Concertos, was recorded in 1995. Why, I ask, did she put herself on the line by choosing such demanding works for her debut album?

"That's another example of something I wasn't really aware of while I was doing it!" she laughs. "I guess it was the innocence of youth.

Andrew Palmer

"Music is so human... the players who can develop relationships with other performers always do better."

Those were the pieces I was performing the most around that time, so I suppose it was inevitable that I should record them.

"Of course, I knew there were lots of other versions available, but I've always believed that it's best to forget about what everyone else is doing. The way to be most free as a performer is to not really care what other people think about you, and to not worry about what others have done in the past. You should focus on what you want to do and then go for it. This is advice that I'd give to every other violinist out there—to every musician, in fact."

Since establishing an international career, Josefowicz has been called upon to collaborate with some of the most highly respected names in the business, not least in the sphere of chamber music. When I ask about the importance of this part of her musical life, she replies without hesitation. "Chamber music is essential. It varies a career and fortifies it. And there's nothing more thrilling than really hitting it off with one of your colleagues." Pianist André Watts is one of her favorite collaborators, and she describes their working relationship as unusually intimate and fulfilling.

She has also established valuable friendships at cellist Truls Mørk's festival in Norway, which she attends every summer. "Last year I did the Kreutzer Sonata there with [pianist] Martha Argerich. That was a real thrill, I can tell you! Her playing was incredible. But you know, what was actually more incredible was communicating with her outside the music, and getting to know her as a person. I must say that when you meet the real personalities out there, you discover that what they do is almost secondary to who they are."

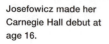

Josefowicz made her Carnegie Hall debut at age 16.

One imagines that Josefowicz's early talent and ambition must have resulted in some feelings of isolation. "I think everyone feels isolated in their own way," she muses, "and you certainly don't have to be a 'star.' We're all human, and we share many of the same feelings. I'm positive of that. I guess the only difference is that I'm well known! But the question of isolation is certainly interesting. I mean, the lifestyle of this whole business is awful. I'll not mince words about that.

"It's not *only* awful, of course. It's great for sightseeing, if you have time. If you don't, then all you see is the hotel rooms, and that's not usually much of a sight. So what you end up truly living for is the music. And that's a big part of my life. But I've discovered in the last few years that it can't be the only part. I won't be satisfied to live only through music. Playing concerts is an intense experience, I must say, but I need as much intensity in my personal life as well."

As with most questions about her early life, Josefowicz's answer has returned the conversation to the present day. Her focus on the here and now highlights the fact that the label of *child prodigy* can stay with a musician for too long, coloring our view of someone who is actually an adult artist. She certainly feels she outgrew that label years ago and is keen to repeat that she's now at a very different stage of her life—physically, mentally, and emotionally. "I'm making a lot of mature decisions these days," she declares proudly.

The intensity she craved in her personal life has come with marriage to conductor Kristjan Järvi, brother of Paavo and son of Neeme. He is currently assistant to Esa-Pekka Salonen, conductor of the Los Angeles Philharmonic. Their home is in New York, but they've recently acquired a second in Florida where, she says, they plan to do most of their "real living" and raise their first child, a son, who is expected soon [Lukas was born in April 2000]. "That's a pretty incredible thing," she smiles, "and it shows how much my life has changed. It's forcing me to take charge and think more seriously about things that I'd otherwise probably let slip, and I'm extremely glad about that."

As Josefowicz enters this new stage of her life, her fans can expect the direction of her career to change. She's already reduced the number of performances she gives and is reevaluating where, what, and with whom she plays. "What really counts," she says, "is playing the pieces that you want to play, in places that matter. That way, it'll seem like you're playing everywhere when you're not! But if you go where anyone asks you to go, and perform repertoire that you're not completely excited about, it won't mean much to you."

Pilavachi declares that Philips has no intention of dragging her into the recording studio against her will. "We've always tried to follow her," he explains, "in the sense that we only record what she's ready to record. That's why you've seen such a variety of repertoire from her. The short encore pieces, the Grieg Sonata, the Messiaen, and Bartók— these are pieces that mean something to her. We knew those discs wouldn't find a huge market, but we have to allow her to develop and grow. There's no rush."

The most noticeable adjustment will be a greater emphasis on 20th-century and contemporary repertoire at the expense of the "classics." Josefowicz is currently preparing John Adams' Violin Concerto for performances next year in Canada and Europe, and she is eager to see the concerto that Estonian composer Erkki-Sven Tüür has just finished. "He didn't compose it specifically for me, but when we play these pieces, we have to pretend they were written for us personally, don't we?" she laughs. "For me, new music is all about giving people an experience in which no predictions are involved. Part of the thrill of going to see a new movie, for example, is that you've never experienced it before; but classical music is often not like that at all.

"Of course, it's interesting to see what different performers can do with something familiar, and I really enjoy playing the standard works. But it's even more interesting to hear something that's only just been

R e c o r d i n g s

Bohemian Rhapsodies. *Sarasate: Carmen Fantasy, Op. 25;*
Zigeunerweisen, Op. 20; Chausson: Poème; Massenet: "Méditation" from
Thaïs; Ravel: Tzigane; Saint-Saëns: Introduction and Rondo Capriccioso,
Op. 28; Wieniawski: Polonaise No. 1. Academy of St. Martin in the
Fields, Sir Neville Marriner, cond. (Philips 454440-2).

For the End of Time. *De Falla: Suite populaire espagnole; Messiaen:*
Quatuor pour la fin du temps, Louange à l'immortalité de Jesus; Grieg:
Sonata No. 3 in C Minor, Op. 45; Bartók: Sonata No. 1. With John
Novacek, piano (Philips 456571-2).

Mendelssohn: Concerto in E minor; Tchaikovsky: Valse-Scherzo, Op. 34;
Glazunov: Concerto in A Minor, Op. 82. Montreal Symphony Orchestra,
Charles Dutoit, cond. (Philips 464059-2).

Solo. Bartók: Sonata; Kreisler: Recitative and Scherzo-Caprice, Op. 6;
Paganini: Introduction and Variations on Nel cor più non mi sento; Ysaÿe:
Sonata in D Minor, Op. 27, No. 3; Sonata for Solo Violin in E Minor, Op.
27, No. 4; Ernst: Le roi des aulnes, Op. 26 (Philips 446700-2).

Tchaikovsky: Concerto in D, Op. 35; Sibelius: Concerto in D Minor.
Academy of St. Martin in the Fields, Sir Neville Marriner, cond. (Philips
446131-2).

Violin for Anne Rice. *Sting: "Moon Over Bourbon Street"; Saint-Saëns:*
Introduction and Rondo Capriccioso, Op. 28; Massenet: "Méditation"
from Thaïs; Sarasate: Carmen Fantasy, Op. 25; Ysaÿe: Sarabande from
Sonata in E Minor, Op. 27, No. 4; Tchaikovsky: Concerto in D, Op. 35;
Sadin: Crescent Moon. Academy of St. Martin in the Fields, Sir Neville
Marriner, cond. (Philips 462032-2).

written, that's just starting to be played. What excites me about contemporary music is that the traditions and rules that governed composition of the 'classics' can't be applied anymore. There are no boundaries to what you can do. Learning a big new piece like the Adams is a huge job, though—you can't assume anything about it, and you can't rely on anything by ear."

There's time for a final question—one that's difficult for any musician to answer. Since Josefowicz declared earlier in our conversation that, for a musician, personality is "absolutely everything," I ask her how she would describe her own. She thinks for a few seconds, then replies, "I guess there's a very outgoing side to me—almost attention-seeking. I mean, those of us who go on stage in front of people have to want a certain amount of attention; otherwise we wouldn't find it enjoyable. There's also an element of looking to take risks—I've been wanting to do this more and more, both personally and professionally, because I don't want to miss out on anything.

"What else can I say? I like to take charge of things, but not by sitting in the driving seat, if you know what I mean. I don't want to be in everyone's face. I prefer to draw people in, have them ask questions, and leave them wanting more!"

And with that, she's off for a meal with her husband, who's flown over from the U.S. to be with her.

Still young, Leila Josefowicz has survived the transition from child prodigy to mature artist. Quietly confident, she nevertheless retains a girlish quality that sits oddly but endearingly with the twin profiles of international virtuoso and mother-to-be. No matter: in both her personal and professional lives, there's much to look forward to. As Costa Pilavachi concludes, "With an artist like her, this is just the beginning."

Nick Briggs/Philips Classics

"What excites me about contemporary music is that the traditions and rules that governed composition of the 'classics' can't be applied anymore."

Joseph Silverstein

Violinist and conductor Joseph Silverstein has had a long and varied career as a performer, teacher, and artistic advisor to numerous orchestras. A native of Detroit, he went to the Curtis Institute in Philadelphia during the 1940s for his formal training. Afterward he played with the Houston and Denver Symphonies and the Philadelphia Orchestra before joining the Boston Symphony Orchestra. During his long tenure there—playing for most of that time as concertmaster—he also became increasingly well known as a conductor, and he went to the Utah Symphony in 1984 to lead that group. This interview was held in 1991; seven years later he stepped down from his full-time career on the podium to become the Utah's conductor laureate. However, he continues to teach and to perform widely as a soloist and chamber musician, and he is a long-time member of the Chamber Music Society of Lincoln Center.

Musician with Many Roles

Edith Eisler

Whether discussing his formative years or his career as a violinist and conductor, Joseph Silverstein radiates a sense of contentment and serenity, and he credits good fortune for most of his achievements with ingenuous modesty. He speaks about other violinists and conductors with what I can only describe as benignity, and he deliberately singles out those on whom he can bestow the highest praise. "In the last few years, a number of really exciting fiddle players have come along," he says. "Take Midori: she is an absolutely delightful, charming young woman, with such superior intelligence that I'm sure she'll play better at 35 than she did at 15. And those who've already been around for a long time are getting better all the time. There are three great violinists on the top level of the international scene, who are less active as soloists than in other roles: Arnold Steinhardt, leader of the Guarneri String Quartet; Schmul Ashkenazi, leader of the Vermeer Quartet; and Jaime Laredo, who has a piano trio, plays a lot of other chamber music, and is also a conductor."

I had heard Silverstein as concertmaster of the Boston Symphony Orchestra (BSO), a post he left in 1984 to become music director of the Utah Symphony. I knew he was a fine violinist, and I was impressed and enchanted by his recent recital in New York. There is something of the old-style virtuoso about him, but without the old-time excesses—never a bad slide or string crossing, nothing cheap or sentimental. He shakes incredible technical feats out of his sleeve and can perform every virtuoso bowing with absolute ease. His tone is sweet and silvery but never cloying; he can get inflection, color, and expression with the slightest change of vibrato or bow pressure. All this is done with the most princely refinement and grace—everything sounds elegant, effortless, and pure.

When he spoke with me last summer at Tanglewood, Silverstein's personal graciousness matched that of his playing. He picked me up and took me to his cottage and arranged a ride for me to his concert in Williamstown, at which he played with the same brilliance and refinement as he had in New York.

Could you tell me something about your training and career?

My father was my first teacher. He was a graduate of the old Institute of Music and Art in New York, which is now the Juilliard School; he taught me until I was 12 years old. At that time, I had the great good fortune that Josef Gingold, that wonderful teacher, came to my hometown of Detroit as concertmaster, and I was one of his first students.

After a year, he felt that it was important for me to go elsewhere, so I was sent to Philadelphia. I played for Efrem Zimbalist in October of 1945, and he took me into the Curtis Institute immediately. I studied with him and also his assistant, Veda Reynolds, for five years, and when I left, I went off to work: to the Houston Symphony Orchestra for three years; to the Philadelphia Orchestra for a year; and to the Denver Symphony as concertmaster and assistant conductor for a year.

During that period, I had the opportunity to learn from my colleagues. In the Houston Symphony, I learned a lot from concertmaster Raphael Fliegel, who is one of the most sophisticated, literate musicians I've ever met in my life, because he reads music so well. [Here, "reading" means paying attention to everything on the page, not sight-reading.] When I came from Curtis, I thought I knew how to read music, but even though I had learned a lot about that from being coached in chamber music by Mr. [William] Primrose, the great violist, it didn't begin to sink in until I saw how this man and Andor Toth, who was assistant concertmaster and assistant conductor, read the music: long notes, short notes, dynamics, rhythms—it was a great education for me.

Then, briefly, I was in the army, and when I came out I had another piece of good fortune: Mischa Mischakoff came to Detroit as concertmaster. I studied with him for a while and also had the pleasure and very inspiring experience of playing in his quartet at the Chautauqua Summer Festival. I feel he was one of the finest violinists of this century. He was an impeccable musician; those years with Toscanini [as concertmaster of the NBC Symphony Orchestra] were great for him. He played with enormous refinement, in the most elegant taste—I have many tapes of his performances.

Then I went to the Boston Symphony, another piece of good fortune. Some of the people in it had studied with Carl Flesch, and some with [Georges] Enesco, and the great Richard Burgin was the concertmaster. He was a grand gentleman and very kind to me; whenever I had anything prepared, I only had to ask if I could play it for him and he was immediately available. His ideas and his information were a treasury, and I learned a great deal from him.

So ever since I've been in the profession, I was able to be around people who were willing to share their very special information with me. The formal teachers I had were wonderful, but I've learned just as much from some of my colleagues.

When did you come to Boston?

In 1955, as the last second violin. And then in 1959 I went to the Queen Elisabeth of Belgium Competition. The orchestra was very gracious in not only allowing but encouraging me to go, and when I came back, the gentleman who was sitting on the third stand, outside, of the first violins decided to retire. We had auditions and [Charles] Munch, who was the conductor at the time, moved me up to that chair. When Munch retired, Burgin also retired, and Erich Leinsdorf came in as the new conductor. He held a rather extended series of auditions, and I was fortunate enough to become concertmaster.

So people do sometimes get advanced from inside the section?

Yes, it happened in the New York Philharmonic with John Corigliano, and also in the Cleveland Orchestra with Daniel Majeski, who of course is a marvelous concertmaster.

Are the first-chair string players in an orchestra really greatly superior to the others?

This is a popular notion, but in the major symphony orchestras now, you find an evenness in the quality of the players that is spectacular. I notice it when I play in chamber-music concerts with members of my own or other orchestras.

What He Plays

Joseph Silverstein play two violins, a Giuseppe Guarneri del Gesù made in 1742 and known as the "ex–Camilla Urso," and a 1773 J.B. Guadagnini called the "ex–Arthur Grumiaux."

"When I played the Tchaikovsky Concerto with the Boston Symphony Orchestra in 1981," Silverstein remembers fondly, "it was the hundredth anniversary of both the concerto and the BSO—and just 100 years before, Urso had played that same del Gesù with the same orchestra!"

Silverstein uses three bows, by Louis Pageot, Dominique Peccatte, and James Tubbs. His strings are Super-Sensitive Sensicores.

What are the special qualifications of a concertmaster, apart from having to be an extremely good player?

It depends on the nature of the orchestra and the particular music director. With conductors like Eugene Ormandy, Lorin Maazel, and Daniel Barenboim, the job is very easy, because they mark all the bowings themselves. You'd expect it with Maazel—he's a wonderful violinist. And Ormandy, I'm told, was a very good one, but Daniel doesn't play the violin at all. Still, not only are his bowings wonderful, he even gives good fingerings.

Where did he learn that?

He's such a smart guy; he's learned it from many people. When George Szell was conductor of the Cleveland Orchestra, he marked the bowings, even with the great Josef Gingold as concertmaster. But with most conductors who are not string players, you have to try to understand their musical philosophy and translate it into the language of the stringed instrument.

I was very fortunate as concertmaster at Boston because we had the Boston Symphony Chamber Players: Mr. [Jules] Eskin [the principal cellist], Mr. [Burton] Fine [the principal violist], and I were playing together all the time, and we had a very good understanding about bowings. I think the most important thing for the concertmaster is to be a musical role model. The conductor William Steinberg said something very interesting to me once: "You play everything longer, shorter, louder, and softer than anybody else." I said I thought that was the job of the concertmaster, and he said, "Exactly, but don't do it too well, because they'll depend on you and let you do all the work for them."

There are many very talented young concertmasters now in the United States, and in four major orchestras, they have been women for about three years: Jorja Fleezanis in Minnesota [see profile beginning on page 37], Cecylia Arzewski in Atlanta, Emmanuelle Boisviert in Detroit, and Nina Bodnar in St. Louis. They are all extraordinarily good; I've conducted these orchestras and very much enjoyed working with them.

This is my first opportunity to talk with someone who has been both a player and a conductor, and there are many things I've wanted to know for ever so long. Surely the sound of an orchestra is produced by the players; how much does the conductor contribute to its unique quality?

I think the conductor has a tremendous effect on the sound. This used to be even more so when there were few guest conductors, and a music director spent a great deal of time with his orchestra. In America, the two with perhaps the most distinctive styles would have been the Cleveland, because for George Szell, the orchestra was his instrument— he knew exactly what he wanted and insisted on getting it—and the Philadelphia, because Eugene Ormandy had a particular sound in mind and hired most of the players himself.

Ormandy, for example, knew what sound he was looking for in every section, and he also enlisted the aid of his solo players when he hired people. So there was an extraordinary consistency during his almost 40 years with the orchestra, even though the personnel changed several times. But they also had great flexibility; when they played with a different conductor, they could assume his identity very quickly.

Rolf Kay

Many guest conductors could achieve this. There was an era of the New York Philharmonic when they were playing with Bruno Walter and Leopold Stokowski; in two successive weeks, you could hear a completely different orchestra with the same personnel. And the first time Ormandy came to the Boston Symphony, within five minutes we sounded like the Philadelphia. Rafael Kubelík got a very rich, dark sound from us, though we were known for our bright one. With him and also with Eugene Jochum, we immediately sounded like a European orchestra.

What's the difference in sound between European and American orchestras?

"The most important thing for the concertmaster is to be a musical role model."

European orchestras tend to be less hard-edged in their attacks, and the strings have more unity of sound. Virtually all the violinists in the Vienna Philharmonic studied in Vienna, and in the Leipzig Gewandhaus Orchestra, most of them studied with the concertmaster.

On the other hand, the woodwinds have a much more distinctive timbre; they really sound different from each other.

Isn't that due to the instruments themselves? The Vienna Philharmonic uses wind instruments that are constructed differently.

It's their whole concept, while the American idea of symphony orchestras was the blending of the woodwind choir, an idea that really started in Philadelphia with Stokowski, who was conductor of the orchestra there from 1912 to 1938.

What you call the "American sound" was really created by European conductors, then, wasn't it?

[*Smiles.*] Well, in those days, there hardly were any others.

How exactly does a conductor manage to affect an orchestra's sound?

Well, I don't know. Something about their physical being, what they are describing with their hands. I don't think the players are even aware of having to make any adjustments. They're responding to the conductor and to the sonority they're hearing around them; good orchestra players know how to become part of a larger unit.

But they still have to remain individually involved with the music. How do they do that, especially the string players?

It's up to the conductor to inspire the whole orchestra to produce the sound and go for a very singular musical result. I think you can see in the gestures of a conductor the description of that certain sound they want, especially in rehearsal. Sir John Barbirolli had a remarkable effect on the sound of the cello section of the BSO; it was radiantly beautiful, perhaps because he was a cellist himself. He used a very long baton and had a seemingly endless legato in his gestures. One cellist remarked, "With him, I feel as if my bow were seven feet long."

When I work with the conducting students here at the Tanglewood Institute, I bring my violin along and ask them to conduct me, and I try to show them by the way I'm producing sound how a violinist's bow will respond to a certain type of beat. The most difficult part of the job is to form in your mind a concept of the music and the sound that is so strong that it can be communicated to the orchestra verbally or physically in such a way that they all want to participate. The conductors I've enjoyed playing with were those with whom I sensed a mutual response, no matter where I was sitting in the section. If a conductor makes you feel that he doesn't know how well you play, it is very discouraging.

Is it easier for a conductor to establish a new orchestra or to take one over, even if he wants to make changes?

It's much easier to deal with a molded unit that's making a statement about sound, ensemble, and articulation. When somebody comes along who has a very strong concept, they can all move together.

Suppose there's disagreement between the new conductor and some of the players?

Well, you have to be somewhat diplomatic. But more often it's a conflict between two players with different personalities. Everyone has a slightly different rhythmic temperament; some are slow players, some fast players, and it's the conductor's job to unify all this. If I have a conceptual problem with a player, I'll discuss it with him privately, not on stage.

How about guest conducting?

That's very easy, because a strange orchestra wants to impress you, and you have to let them know how good they are. So there's a sort of wonderful, quick seduction going on.

Suppose a guest wants the orchestra to adopt a style that's completely alien to them?

Well, then the musicians fight it, and the result isn't too happy. But that only happens rarely, because they know that next week you'll be gone. As music director, however, you are dealing on a long-range basis with

Recordings

Barber: *Violin Concerto.* Utah Symphony Orchestra, C. Ketchum, cond. (Pro Arte CDD 241).

Beach: *Music for Violin and Piano.* With V. Eskin, piano (Northeastern NOR 9004).

Beethoven: *Septet.* With the Chamber Music Society of Lincoln Center (Delos DE 3177).

Beethoven: *Violin Concerto, Op. 61.* Utah Symphony Orchestra, Joseph Silverstein, cond. and soloist (Pro Arte CDD 288).

Beethoven: *Violin Concerto, Op. 61; Die Weihe des Hauses.* Utah Symphony Orchestra, Joseph Silverstein, cond. and soloist (Pro Arte CDS 588).

Brahms: *Violin Concerto.* Utah Symphony Orchestra, Joseph Silverstein, cond. and soloist (Pro Arte CDD 271).

Brahms: *Violin Concerto.* Utah Symphony Orchestra, C. Ketchum, cond. (Pro Arte CDS 3431).

Dohnányi: *Serenade; Kodály: Serenade for Two Violins and Viola.* With Ani Kavafian, violin; Gary Hoffman, cello; and Paul Neubauer, viola (Delos DE 3151).

Dvořák: *Violin Concerto.* Utah Symphony Orchestra, Joseph Silverstein, cond. and soloist (Pro Arte CDD 389).

Foote: *Pieces for Violin and Piano, Op. 9; Trio No. 2.* With V. Eskin, piano; Jules Eskin, cello (Northeastern NOR 206).

Korngold and Schmidt: *Music for Strings and Piano Left Hand.* With Leon Fleischer, piano; Joseph Silverstein, Jamie Laredo, Joel Smirnoff, violins; Michael Tree, viola; Yo-Yo Ma, cello (Sony Classical 7464-48253-2).

Mendelssohn: *Violin Concerto, Op. 64.* Utah Symphony Orchestra, Joseph Silverstein, cond. and soloist (Pro Arte CDD 187).

Mozart: *Sonatas for Violin and Piano.* With Derek Han, piano (Verdi Classics 5-VMS 6815).

Music of Grieg. Grieg: *Peer Gynt Suites 1 and 2; Holberg Suite; Piano Concerto, First Movement.* With Russell Sherman, piano; Utah Symphony Orchestra, A. Gerhardt, cond. London Promenade Orchestra (Pro Arte CDM 811).

Music of Mendelssohn. Mendelssohn: Violin Concerto in E, Op. 64; Midsummer Night's Dream Overture; and others. Houston Symphony Orchestra, S. Comissiona, cond.; Utah Symphony Orchestra (Pro Arte CDM 815).

Schubert: Octet. With the Boston Chanber Players (Elektra/Nonesuch 79046-2).

Schuman, Clara: Piano Trio. With Colin Carr, cello; Veronica Jochum, piano (Tudor TUD 788).

Tchaikovsky: Swan Lake. With Jules Eskin, cello; Armando Ghitalla, trumpet; Bernard Zighera, harp; Boston Symphony Orchestra, Seiji Ozawa, cond. (Deutsche Grammophon 2-453055-2)

Vivaldi: Violin Concertos Nos. 1-4, Op. 8; The Four Seasons. Boston Symphony Orchestra, Seiji Ozawa, cond. (Telarc CD 80070, CS 30070).

people whom you have to impress with your level of preparation, by saying fresh things about pieces they've played before, and by working very hard to get them more money and raise their status in the community.

How does a conductor get experience? He needs a whole orchestra to practice on.

Certainly not by standing in front of the mirror with a record, but by being assistant conductor or apprentice with a great musician, by watching others, and observing himself. I feel that the best schools are those where the conductors have to play in the orchestra. When a conductor like Lorin Maazel, or Colin Davis, who was a fine clarinetist, stands in front of you, there's a sense that he knows what it's like to sit down with you. And the pianists who conduct well are good chamber-music players; James Levine, for example, is superb—I've played with him. But it takes time, and it's unfair and irrational to expect young conductors to perform in as mature a way as young instrumentalists; one can't spend as many hours with an orchestra as with an instrument.

Tell me more about the Boston Symphony Chamber Players.

It was formed in 1963, while Erich Leinsdorf was the conductor. At that time, the BSO, like many other major orchestras, was going to the full-year contract. Before that, the BSO had the winter season, the Pops had the spring, and there was Tanglewood during the summer, and since the solo players never played the Pops, it was necessary to offer them employment in the spring. With the cooperation of the conductor, the manager, and the chairman of the board, we decided that the Chamber Players would go on tour in the spring, and during the winter season we would play three or four concerts in Boston and possibly New York. We would prepare new repertoire for each of these concerts, so that we would have something fresh to record and to take on the road each year. I think it was the first time in the country that you could have performances all in one house of such pieces as the Beethoven Septet, the Schubert Octet, and the Spohr Nonet, which ordinarily had to be assembled with players from here, there, and everywhere. We concentrated on the combined wind-and-string repertoire; it was a unique opportunity. Of course, we made many records, and I'm very proud of them—I think they are examples of a very high level of chamber music because we were working together all the time.

Did you rehearse all year?

Well, over the course of the season, though certainly with more intensity just prior to performances.

Why did you leave Boston and go to Utah?

It really almost came by surprise. I loved being concertmaster of the Boston Symphony and I enjoyed the Chamber Players, but I began to be invited as guest conductor and guest soloist with many other orchestras, and it was very difficult for me to get the time off because, after all, I had a major responsibility! I had been with the orchestra for almost 30 years and was concertmaster for well over 20. I was still under contract in Boston when it turned out that I was the choice of the Utah search committee; I went there and explored the situation, and it was very exciting.

A very happy consequence that I didn't expect has been all the solo playing and guest conducting I do now. As you know, in our profession you develop a certain identity, and people don't like to see you assume another one, so when I left the BSO, many people thought I wasn't going to play any more. But that was never my intention. On the contrary, at this point I think I can maintain my playing more easily, because I am playing only for myself. With the BSO, I had to practice after playing five hours of rehearsal; now, when I come home, I haven't been using my hands on the violin, so I have that energy and a sense of freshness, which is great fun. Next winter, I'll be playing 11 different concertos, two recital programs, and a lot of chamber music, so I'm really very much involved with both conducting and the violin. I don't feel one is taking precedence over the other, and I'm having a wonderful time.

Do you also play solo with your own orchestra?

Oh yes, we've made lots of recordings, and I play with the orchestra at least once a year. When we toured in Europe, I played many times. In short, what caused me to leave the BSO was the desire to do more solo playing and conducting. Besides, with our children grown up, it became practical to travel together with my wife, which would have been impossible before. I don't even feel any need to take vacations; there's so much variety to my work that I want to do as much as possible. I loved playing with the BSO, but I love what I'm doing now even more.

Jorja Fleezanis

Jorja Fleezanis, concertmaster of the Minnesota Orchestra since 1989, is an active teacher, chamber musician, and soloist. In addition to performing the standard solo and orchestral repertoire with analytical passion, she is also intensely interested in contemporary music. She has commissioned and premiered numerous contemporary works by such composers as Aaron Jay Kernis and John Adams, and in 1999 she gave the British premiere of Nicholas Maw's Sonata for Solo Violin, which was commissioned for her by Minnesota Public Radio.

In this 1997 interview, Fleezanis talks insightfully about the challenges and joys of making music as the leader of a group—in, as she puts it, a "community of like souls."

A Part of the Whole

Russell Platt

When I meet up with Jorja Fleezanis at Minneapolis' Orchestra Hall on a brisk October day, she is stricken with a bad cold— acquired, as is typical of particularly active people, just as she is taking a much-deserved week off.

Fleezanis is a busy woman. In addition to holding the position of concertmaster of the Minnesota Orchestra (which she has held since 1989, when conductor Edo de Waart brought her out from the associate concertmaster's desk at the San Francisco Symphony), Fleezanis teaches violin privately and at the University of Minnesota, and she enjoys active side careers as an orchestra soloist, chamber musician, and contemporary-music champion. The Twin Cities' classical-music community is a tight-knit one in which Fleezanis plays a central role; she is also a pleasant refutation of the particularly American notion of gaining personal fulfillment through the mad pursuit of media stardom. A woman of considerable breadth of learning as well as intense musicality, she is clearly a musician who likes to share as much as she leads, though she leads orchestras with a passion. The continuing success of the Minnesota Orchestra under controversial music director Eiji Oue depends mightily on the discipline of Fleezanis, who has been a faithful steward of the orchestra's sumptuous string sound, most notably developed in recent times by the MO's early-'80s maestro Neville Marriner.

Lisa Kohler

"You're just as much a chamber music player when you're in an orchestral setting."

Fleezanis is an artist who, in middle age, has matured like a fine vintage. She began her studies with Ara Zerounian in Detroit, where she was born, and continued at Interlochen, Meadowbrook, the Cleveland Institute of Music, and the Cincinnati College-Conservatory of Music. She joined the Chicago Symphony at 23 but left to form the Trio d'Accordo and to become concertmaster of the Cincinnati Chamber Orchestra, betraying an independent streak that would continue through the years. More recently she has formed the FOG trio with pianist Garrick Ohlsson and San Francisco Symphony principal cellist Michael Grebanier, served as guest concertmaster for Roger Norrington and the London Classical Players, and soloed not only with the Minnesota Orchestra but with the San Francisco, New World, Baton Rouge, and Toledo Symphonies. She also teaches and performs frequently at the Round Top Festival in Texas. She has been one of the canniest contemporary musicians around, providing forceful advocacy for such composers as Roger Sessions and Ellen Taaffe Zwilich, as well as premiering works such as Aaron Jay Kernis' *Brilliant Sky, Infinite Sky* and, most important, the Violin Concerto of John Adams.

That work's debut was a stunning showcase for Fleezanis' muscular style of playing. Her tone is full and intense, but I suspect she is uninterested in pursuing beauty of sound for its own sake. My brother, conductor Alexander Platt, collaborated with her last fall [1996] in a performance of the Samuel Barber Violin Concerto with the Marion Philharmonic in Indiana, and he backed up that idea, saying, "I admired how she drew out the lyricism of the concerto through pacing and tempo relations rather than through just a generalized prettiness." That comment reveals a signal quality in Fleezanis' playing and general musical outlook: responsibility to the score, an investigatory, thorough approach that seeks to relate to the entire musical fabric, not just to deliver a polished account of the solo part. Her marriage to eminent musicologist and critic Michael Steinberg seems wonderfully apt, since he shares her broad interests, catholic taste, and positive musical viewpoint.

I don't know of a leading violinist who's more eclectic than you are in musical interests and professional roles. How did it all start?

As I developed as a musician, I got the opportunity to "taste test" everything. In my public-school experience I had a private teacher who met with me individually for the solo repertoire, but he had me playing string quartets very early, and I was very serious about it. I was doing Beethoven's Op. 18, No.1, at age 13 and Op. 59, No. 3, at 15, both with very good groups. So chamber music was like mother's milk to me. But I was also playing in orchestras from the beginning: school orchestras, civic orchestras, summer camp.

I was lucky in my education in that at no time did a mentor say, "You can only do *this*." Probably the most important and demanding of my early teachers was Mischa Mischakoff, then concertmaster of the Detroit Symphony, and former concertmaster of the NBC Symphony. He was a giant of an instrumentalist, and he wanted his students to play like soloists, with those solo instincts, those muscles. But he wanted us to be ensemble players, too—so solo work always radiated out to the other facets of being a musician.

The other big thing was working at the Meadowbrook summer orchestral institute in Michigan with [conductor] James Levine. This was an orchestral institute in every sense of the word; that's what you were there for. It was intense, but I ate it up. It just happened that another role model in that little enclave was Lynn Harrell, a very close friend of Levine's. He was a magnetic pole for us—he was young but in the profession, the pull toward your next chapter in life. He was principal cellist of the Cleveland Orchestra then, and he was an example of someone who wasn't exclusively a soloist: for him it wasn't a question of playing in an orchestra or not; it was a question of *playing music*. He had to play everything, the Beethoven and Brahms symphonies, and he played them in a way that brought out everything he would use in the Elgar Cello Concerto. He taught us that when you're playing in an orchestra you're in a very challenging ensemble situation that deals in the same issues that you deal with in a Beethoven string quartet; you have to learn the same skills.

You often hear of musicians who get bored with playing in orchestras, feeling that they're just there to carry out the conductor's orders. You obviously don't think that way. It's not too different from being a soloist?

Well, it is different from being a soloist, but it's not "discount" music making. You are in a community of like souls. If you have any pride in yourself on how to make a phrase, you're in charge of that phrase—but you can't make it independent of the section. You have to be able to play with your colleagues, and you have to understand what the phrase is. Students think of the great composers' symphonies as lesser things than their concertos and sonatas; they're not being encouraged to look at those orchestral parts with the same aesthetics and maturity as those

What She Plays

Jorja Fleezanis plays a Lorenzo Storioni instrument from late 18th-century Cremona and a Dominique Peccatte bow from mid-19th-century France. Also, she plays Bach and some Classical music on a transitional bow by the Dodd family of makers of early 19th-century England.

Fleezanis has been a guest concertmaster for the London Classical Players under Roger Norrington, and she used gut strings for the occasion. "In Wagner, playing with gut strings changed the whole way to make a phrase happen," she says. "Especially with a gut E, the color and subtlety of nuance changes the way you approach the music. I'm fascinated by the idea that left-hand vibrato wasn't omnipresent then; resultingly, the bow had to be much more expressive, not through pressure, but to get 'speed' into the sound, getting the resonance of the instrument to affect phrase shape. And this affects tempos."

At the time of this interview, Fleezanis used Dominant G and D strings and a Corelli E string, and she was "experimenting" with a Tonica A. She currently uses a Wondertone/Pirastro E, a Larsen A and D, and an Olive G.

Recordings

Bolle: Eight Pieces. With Basil Reeve, oboe (Gasparo 317).

Wolpe: Violin Sonata. With Garrick Ohlsson, piano (Koch International Classics 7112).

Kernis: Love Scenes. With Sanford Sylvan, baritone; Daniel Dreuckman, percussion; Robert Helps, piano.

pieces that are closest to their egos. If anything, it's even more challenging to play those phrases and cadences in an orchestra, in one breath. That collectiveness is what makes the orchestra a powerful place to express yourself—but you have to see it that way. You can't think, "I am anonymous"—you have to say, "I am proud of this orchestra and of this section, and this is great music."

I remember all those books of orchestral excerpts from my days as a young violinist. It's as if the profession is saying, "This is all you need." What you're talking about is knowing the score.

Yes, you're just as much a chamber music player when you're in an orchestral setting.

It seems so many musicians are content to be compartmentalized in the corporate musical structure we have today: you're an orchestral player, soloist, conductor, composer, critic, academic, or whatever. There's so little overlap. It wasn't always this way.

I've worked with some mavericks: Christoph Eschenbach, a conductor and a fine pianist; Michael Tilson Thomas, a conductor, pianist, and composer; and Joseph Silverstein—another big role model—a conductor and violin soloist who was also a concertmaster [see profile beginning on page 25].

"You can sense those people who are strong within themselves but are part of the community."

A term I find myself using these days is "holistic" as an approach to music. Until I was 35, I felt a little bit out of balance in pulling things together. It was kind of a crisis: I felt that my body and the way I played needed to have a kind of synergy. Finding it came from dealing with my internal world, and also with Alexander Technique, which I started doing then, in San Francisco. That led to being aware of all aspects of being a musician, of not being myopic, of bringing all my experience as a musician into everything I'm doing, all the time. Maybe this is complex—but when I'm a concerto soloist, I just can't *think* I'm that, I have to be aware of those muscles working, the same ones I'd use as an orchestral player. You project more sound and volume, but you've still got to be part of the whole. It all just has to do with understanding music. And that's what separates a lot of the people who come to play with orchestras. You can sense those people who are strong within themselves but are part of the community.

Do you believe the obsession with worldly success can be destructive?

It's a horribly destructive way of leading your life. Who's to say what success is, in personal expression? I'm just committed to the idea of re-creation, of reinterpretation. You're the one actually igniting a piece, but the performer has to be humbled by the composer. It's a relationship that demands total faithfulness to the manuscript, to the extent that it's possible.

The piece is your teacher.

The piece is your teacher! Again, by sheer chance I had teachers who taught that way, and so I don't think it's complete to teach from the instrument—but you have to be totally familiar with it, fascinated with its physics, its potential, like the most gifted craftsman.

Does this carry into your teaching?

In a big way. I have two full-time students, a third who commutes, and then a lot of people who come for tune-ups, tune-ins. . . . I enjoy that work: I'm good at focusing people on their body, soul, and mind. That can't be avoided; it's paramount. If a person is uptight, physically in knots, they're just not going to be able to get it out. It's *internal*. They can move the shoulder, do this, do that, but if they're still playing like a clam, I say, "Sing it out; vocalize it from the gut." A long-range mission of mine is to develop a curriculum that combines early physical awareness with vocal training, which really gets you to understand how to sing a phrase, *before* you play the instrument.

I didn't have any of that at conservatory, but at the Cleveland Institute I was again with Jimmy Levine and Lynn Harrell; the Style and Interpretation course was a direct offshoot of Meadowbrook. We would go through the Schubert *Winterreise, Die schöne Müllerin*—it taught me how to *covet the score*. It's like anything in life. If you just choose one strand of something out of 50 strands, you'll just have one strand; it's not too interesting after ten minutes, unless you're really Zen-oriented. . . .

Maybe for some people that's enough, that's their natural path?

But in the orchestra you have to constantly be aware: of how to accompany, of what's in the horn parts. It's responsibility to the whole. It's not on a moral level, it's just more *interesting*, it keeps you alive to the idea that a hundred people are all doing this together. Going into your section and being oblivious to what's going on around you does not make for a good orchestra. And I can tell this in auditions: it's instantly apparent who knows the score, who's aware of an accompanimental part underneath, who understands what goes on to the last moment of a whole note.

I guess it's no accident you married a musicologist! [Laughter.]

I used to think about that a lot, but I guess we just gravitate to like minds. One of the early moments that fused us together was at a Thanksgiving dinner with some people in the San Francisco Symphony. We had all just had turkey, we were all blissed out, sitting on the floor listening to the Budapest Quartet play Haydn . . . I suddenly realized that [he and I] were anticipating the moments in the same way, that we were reacting in the same way.

Do you prepare pieces together?

No. Probably because of my pride and my own curiosity, my independent investigation is critical—that's what I take on stage. But I'm aware
that I have a terrific resource in him. We talk about music *all* the time,
the profession, who's just performing and who's performing *music*. But
I'm careful how much I rely on him.

*You've done so much contemporary music, and by some important
composers. Is it always helpful to have the composer in on the rehearsal
process?*

It can be unhelpful, or disarming. I played Elliott Carter's *Riconoscenza
per Goffredo Petrassi* [for solo violin], and he was very sweet with me. I'd
played the piece before, but when I saw him in the audience I thought,
"Here's where every hole, every misguided thought on this piece, will be
brought out!" When you're in front of a composer, you realize that they
are totally dependent on you: you're translating *your* expressiveness
through *their* language. It's something they themselves cannot do, so it
becomes a symbiosis in the best sense. It's my job to find out where they
want the piece to go.

Sometimes they don't know!

Sometimes they don't! But it's a door, and we have to find out what's on
the other side.

*You've been incredibly broad in your choice of new-music repertoire.
Even though we're in the '90s now and everything's happy and "diverse"
[laughter] and the tonal-atonal wars are over, there are still factions, or
schools. Composers are passionate people, and they disagree on things,
but you've avoided all this. Where do you think music is going?*

Well, I don't find that the schools are any of my business, frankly. I'm
interested in the human creator, if the craft and the expression are
fused, if it's honest. The greatness of what's out there creates me, in a
way. I respond to it and I become wiser, bigger, more capable as a result.
I can remember when I started learning the Sessions Violin Concerto. If
I'd talked to five different people about it, they'd have said, "Why are
you learning this? No one's gonna like it; it'll be a drag on you," and I
never would have learned it.

Sessions was a hell of a composer, but his music is tough to like.

You have to really love it, love what these composers are saying, not just
learn the nuts and bolts. That's why this music is often written off,
because people feel it's not expressive. So it's important for the musician
to be in touch with that expression at all times. Anything that's calling
itself music has got to be expressive—even electronic tones, if they're
collected in such a way, as in [Milton] Babbitt, that there's balance, pro-
portion, pitch relation. I remember hearing one of the big [Pierre]

Boulez pieces for orchestra, listening with an open mind. If I felt lost, it was when I felt that the objective was to get these people to play as electronically as possible, as though they were a living computer. It was dazzling, but it was really uncomfortable for me . . . but I've been part of some pretty wild things. I remember playing something of Babbitt's with tape, and thinking, "This really is *challenging,* something that sharpens your ability to do things rhythmically"—whether or not it made me play Brahms better. It must have affected me in some way.

A piece like the Barber Concerto, on the other hand, is easy to love. It's as if [opera composer Giacomo] Puccini wrote a violin concerto! The melodic inspiration is absolutely top-drawer. But when I first started playing it, in 1988, hardly anybody knew it. It was ridiculous; this is the most user-friendly, comfy piece. I thought, I do other lush, beautiful pieces; why not this? You can sing in this piece, express yourself.

What makes it challenging?

It's very challenging to play those first two movements, and then draw that maniacal side out of yourself on a dime—you've got to be cool when that timpani starts off. It's these contrasts that keep me vibrant, the ability to step into these roles quickly; it's what makes great actors, that presence of mind.

In closing, I'd like to ask you how you would guide students in these difficult times for classical music.

There have never been any guarantees; don't just look at the violin. It takes many hours to be a master, hours of those études and scales—and to be imaginative and creative, even in that work. Never play outside yourself, always draw from within. So you have to be able to understand everything that's going on in the music you're playing; read as much as you can about it. Listen to old recordings of pieces, musicians like [German violinist and composer] Adolf Busch, [Hungarian/American violinist] Joseph Szigeti—these people were busy, but they had time to saturate themselves, they *understood* the late Beethoven quartets; they had an ability to be more comprehensive and curious about music in general.

I want my students to see the richness of their art form, to go to operas, plays, read books, tie things in so that their cultural awareness is very broad. I'm not interested creating soloists; I'd like people to become good ensemble players—which means when they're learning a sonata, they learn the piano score as well, so they're *never* playing in a vacuum. Learning to be a component of a larger whole. That's the kind of highway I open up.

I'm also big on drama: I'd like players who work with me to have custody of their dramatic personae, and, like a great singer or actor, that they take a piece of music and see it as a script. I often teach that way: "What do you see in this script? What are the nuances of your lines, the other characters?" Anything to get them out of feeling it's just fourth finger, up bow. . . .

We have no control of the future. But I'm in it right now; I'm actively involved as a go-between, with the conductor, the orchestra, the board, the public. It's how I get people interested in what I'm doing down at Orchestra Hall—it's not enough to say, "Come down and see me play." I also do coaching in public schools, a lot of hands-on stuff. The number of people I might see in a year—it's a *lot* of people. I have to express why it's *worthwhile*.

The experience of music is neutral, and yet so profound: it's about us, and yet it's not tangible. If it comes from the core of the performer, the voice of the creator, then you're getting a line that's one of the most powerful ways of drawing us together—and I've never known music to pull people apart. There's a spiritual bonding that goes on in concert halls: the intense way in which everyone is one *thing*, one *pulse*, and it's all focusing through the incredible devotion to the performer to this moment. When I think of how shallowly so many students are put in touch with this—the way the profession and the media distract us from what this is all about is unfortunate. But we'll probably always gravitate to music, because it's at a sheer primal level, and yet it takes us so much higher than we could ever go without it.

Viktoria Mullova

The compelling Russian violinist Viktoria Mullova has had an intriguing career that has brought her numerous awards (including a Grand Prix du Disque, Diapason d'Or, Grammy, and Deutsche Schallplattenkritik). Her personal life has been equally eventful—she made a dramatic defection from the Soviet Union in 1983 and quickly established a professional career outside the Iron Curtain (she now lives in London).

As a child, Mullova studied at Moscow's Central Music School and at the Moscow Conservatory, and she first captured international attention in 1980, when she won first prize at Helsinki's Sibelius Competition. Two years later she won the Gold Medal at the Tchaikovsky Competition in Moscow.

Now she has expanded her career beyond solo renditions of the classics: in 1994 she launched the Mullova Chamber Ensemble, which tours and records in a historically authentic style. And as this book goes to press she is completing a tour with the Orchestra of the Age of Enlightenment, acting for the first time as both soloist and director (a project she refers to in this 1998 interview). She is also venturing into the nonclassical realm with a forthcoming Philips recording entitled Through the Looking Glass, *a collection of arrangements of works by Miles Davis, Duke Ellington, the Beatles, Yousou N'Dour, Alanis Morissette, and others.*

The Individualist

Andrew Palmer

Astonishing though a finely honed technique undoubtedly is, there's an aspect of musicianship that's more remarkable and even more precious: individuality. Even in the best-known work, an artist of

Viktoria Mullova's caliber reminds you immediately *whom*, as well as *what*, you're listening to. Her uniqueness is difficult to sum up in a few words, but one can begin to describe why she's such a thrilling performer by pointing out her muscularity of tone, her directness of interpretation, and her sometimes disquieting blend of aggression and playfulness. All musicians are unique, but Mullova seems even more so than most.

Sasha Gusov

"When I'm playng, I'm trying to put my feelings into music."

Which partially explains why the prospect of interviewing her produces some apprehension. Soloists inevitably acquire a public persona, and the popular perception of Mullova tends to be of a cerebral ice queen—passionate, certainly, but tough rather than romantic, gritty rather than warm. Yet there also lurks the suspicion that such a generalized image must surely reflect only part of her character, and that in real life she's as open and friendly as the next person. The truth, as always, lies somewhere between the two extremes.

Her physical appearance is certainly a surprise. Publicity photos tend to portray her as sunny but slightly delicate and waiflike; in contrast, the woman who opens her door to me is taller and more powerfully built than I'd expected. Home is an Edwardian terraced house in southwest London, where she lives with her two young children, and even though she's awaiting the imminent arrival of Number Three and looking the picture of casual domesticity, she has a striking physical presence. Her features are static, even severe, and mesmerizing.

She leads me to the living room, past a child's bike hanging from one of the walls in the entrance hall, and while she makes coffee I take in the surroundings. Plainly but not sparsely decorated, the room has a polished wooden floor, simple but substantial furniture, and large works of abstract art, predominantly in blues and grays, on each wall. It's all very smart, cool, discerning, and professional—presumably a reflection of its occupant's character.

Before serious conversation begins, there's a confession: during my research I couldn't find a single recent interview feature about her in the British press. "Good," she says, smiling. "They write silly things about you." Coffee is then poured in silence, and I begin to realize that she'll be making many of her statements through understatement. There's no reason, of course, that anyone should give an interview simply for the pleasure of talking about themselves to a complete stranger, but the fact remains that many musicians do just that. For Mullova, the process is presumably one to be endured rather than enjoyed.

Putting aside the immediate question of why she's agreed to talk to me, I ask about her childhood in Russia. She was born in Moscow in

November 1959, the eldest of four children, and started to play the violin at the age of four. "My parents wanted me to learn an instrument," she explains in quiet, measured tones. "They weren't musical, but their ambition was for me to play the violin. We had only one room for all six of us, so there was no space for a piano." Like all Russian children, she started school at the age of seven. Two years later she was accepted by the Central Music School, part of the Moscow Conservatory, and for the following nine years she studied with Volodar Bronin, himself a former pupil of David Oistrakh.

Did she have anything like a normal childhood? "Yes and no. Of course I had less time to go out and play with other kids. But I used to go on holiday with my parents, and when I was nine years old we went up into the Caucasus mountains for one month—without the violin, which was very, very strange. But a whole month up there was a great experience. So yes, I used to do things that most other people do."

What most other children wouldn't have done, however, was make a concerto debut at the age of 12. That was in Gorky in 1972, playing a Viotti concerto, and she returned a few months later to perform Vieuxtemps' Fifth. Whether or not Mullova's parents had anticipated the true extent of their daughter's musical talent, their hopes for her were being amply rewarded. "They were very supportive," she recalls, "and they encouraged me all the time. And because I started to play better and better, and obviously was doing better than the other kids, this made me practice even harder and achieve even more."

Mullova clearly acknowledges the influence of her parents, but her comments don't reveal the extent of their extraordinary dedication to her future career. These two educated but unmusical people not only dared to dream of a future for their daughter as a professional musician, but also set about helping her to achieve that dream. Mullova's father, an engineer, attended many of her violin lessons, making notes about her performance, and afterward they would discuss technical details at home. It wasn't unusual for the young Viktoria—still a child—to practice for several hours a day under his guidance. Her mother, a schoolteacher, was similarly committed to her future and took her, at the age of ten, to observe the auditions for the 1970 Tchaikovsky Competition. As for her brother and twin sisters, "they started to play piano but they didn't develop it into anything much," says Mullova. "I think my parents' energy was all used up on me!"

Before long, Bronin confirmed that she was destined for a professional career. At 18 she accordingly moved up to the Moscow Conservatory, where she studied with Leonid Kogan, and two years later she won first prize in the 1980 Sibelius Competition in Helsinki. I ask about her memories of that event. "Well, it wasn't actually my first competition—that was one in Holland for younger players, when I was 16, and I won that too. It wasn't a major competition, like the Sibelius. *That* was very hard."

What She Plays

Mullova's instrument is nowhere to be seen during the interview, and in fact there are few obvious signs that her home is a musical one. When questioned, she reveals that her violin is the "Julius Falk" Antonio Stradivari of 1723.

"I got it in April 1985, and I was really very lucky because soon afterward the prices shot up," she says. "It was bought at Sotheby's in London with the help of a Russian musical foundation. That was a huge help to me, and I have since been able to pay them back."

The history of the instrument can be traced virtually without a break. It was almost certainly one of 11 violins the celebrated Florentine collector Count Cozio di Salabue bought directly from Stradivari's son Paolo after the maker's death. The dealer Luigi Tarisio bought it from the count and later, on his first trip to Paris, sold it to J.B. Vuillaume. He in turn sold it to the French violinist (and pupil of Kreutzer) Paul Vidal. After Vidal's death, the instrument was acquired by the French dealers Gand & Bernardel for three successive clients, the last of whom was the American Jules Falk. He died in 1957, and two years later his brother Charles bought the violin from his estate.

"Everybody asks me why I never change the instrument, or why I don't have two instruments like many violinists," Mullova says. "But actually, I don't see why I should. I already have everything I need. Besides, playing a different instrument takes so much getting used to. I know my Strad so well—it's a part of me."

Mullova's bow is an F.N. Voirin that she's had for about nine years. She emphasizes that she's recently started using gut strings for Bach and Mozart, and she says that the differences in the sound produced and the sensation of playing on them are amazing. "Gut strings change completely the interpretation that I give. The way I make a sound, or a phrase, is completely different. You can't put gut strings on and just play in the same way; it's absolutely impossible. It's like playing another violin."

Mullova, of course, belongs to a generation of musicians for whom competitions have been a way of life. But she points out that in the Russia of the early 1980s, winning awards was critical to professional success. "For us there was no choice. At 13 it was absolutely impossible to start a career without winning something, and so people like Kremer and Spivakov went off to play in as many competitions as possible. It was the only opportunity you had to get out. If you didn't succeed, there probably wouldn't be another chance. So there was a very big pressure to win. And most important, to win the first prize. The Tchaikovsky Competition [in Moscow, at which she won the Gold Medal in 1982] was the most difficult of all. Everybody knows this, because it's a very prestigious event. And I must say that the greatest competition in the Tchaikovsky is between Russians. You have to win [first place] to succeed."

Sasha Gusov

This desire among Russian musicians to leave their country may have been widespread, but it was also often unspoken. While her practicing, performing, and competing continued, the 22-year-old Mullova was secretly making her own plans to get out. "I prepared for a long time—a year—to leave, and I kept it very quiet. I knew

Mullova made a concerto debut at the age of 12.

that I could play the violin, and I thought there would be lots of opportunities for me in the West. I knew that it would be better than the Soviet Union, for sure. But I wasn't thinking about managing a career or making recordings, and in fact I didn't even know how it worked in the West. I had no idea. For me the most important thing was to escape and to be free—as a human being, not just as a musician. And I had this feeling that I could be all right."

Her parents had pushed her down a narrow and demanding path, and it's possible that part of the freedom she craved was to have more personal and physical space away from them. Whatever the reason, she kept her plans secret from her family, and what happened next came as a great shock to them. She speaks today about the big event of 1983 with scarcely more emotion than if she were describing the purchase of a new violin; yet the fact remains that, while on a tour of Scandinavia, she walked into the U.S. Embassy in Stockholm and requested political asylum. "Yes, I defected," she confirms.

Costa Pilavachi, then-president of the Philips Music Group in Amsterdam [now president of Universal Music, Philips' parent company], has known Mullova since 1984. He was involved with her very first recording, the Tchaikovsky and Sibelius Concertos, with the Boston Symphony and Seiji Ozawa, and he understands why her account of defecting is so dispassionate. "It used to be the only topic of conversation with interviewers," he points out. "She's probably gone over it so many times that she doesn't get excited about it anymore."

Sasha Gusov

Once in the West, Mullova spent two years in Washington, D.C., before deciding to move to Europe: first to Italy, then Vienna, and finally London. She succeeded in creating a solo career and later also started a family. I suggest that it must be difficult to balance the demands of motherhood with a career. "Oh, it's very easy," she says. "My son was born while I was traveling everywhere, so I just took him to all my concerts. Then my daughter arrived and there were two children, but soon afterward my son started school, so I just took her with me. Now they both go to the same school and the third one will be traveling with me. So it's possible to organize your travels and performing around children. My daughter, who's three now, came to hear one of my concerts recently and sat there singing all through my performance!"

Turning to the subject of Mullova's image as a performer, I explain to her that as part of my research I've read several reviews of her performances and have been struck by how frequently her playing is described in words like "tough" or "steely." One critic mentions her "conscious refusal to prettify music. . . . She adopts a weightier, more aggressive tone than most." Another, noting that her playing shines with a "glint of platinum," writes of an "immaculately considered and technically flawless but humorless performance." And another of a performance "purged of Romantic excess." "If only she let that warmth invade her playing more often," the critic continues, "she would be unbeatable." Does this imply that she has a natural aversion to romanticism?

Mullova has the magnetism of someone who gives away sufficiently little of herself to leave you hungry for more.

A flicker of agitation passes across her face, and she suddenly becomes more animated. "First of all," she replies, "if people write something about you in an interview it doesn't mean that it's right. And secondly, you can't just take the words of a reviewer out of the context. You have to know what he's speaking about, what kind of composer it is. I like a romantic sound, and in Brahms and Tchaikovsky it *has* to be romantic. It cannot be dry. It's a completely different feeling, completely different emotions. If I don't do vibrato in Mozart and Bach the sound is more pure, but to me it's still extremely romantic."

She has a point. When quoting reviews one should include positive as well as negative comments; she has been praised for her "strength of purpose yet athletic but subtle grace," and her disc of the Mendelssohn E-Minor Concerto has been named "among the finest concerto recordings of our time." She's also right about not taking words out of context.

Nevertheless, I'm intrigued by the level of consensus among her critics. Each one describes her playing in a similar way, and together they paint a consistent picture of an artist who's not necessarily "difficult" but . . . uncompromising, perhaps. One who doesn't try to persuade an audience with her music so much as simply present it to them. "The music, how it is, how it's written, how it should be, and how I feel it," Mullova puts it succinctly.

I try a more conciliatory tack, deciding to risk comparing her to a singer like Maria Callas. "Yes," she nods eagerly. A singer who isn't afraid to make an ugly sound if it suits the drama of the music? "Yes, yes. When I'm playing, I'm trying to put my feelings into music. I have my own convictions of how it should be played. I'm not doing it to please the public; it's just the way I feel this music. I can't play it in a different way."

This sounds reasonable, and I wonder afterward whether I've been unduly influenced by other writers' perceptions of her. Is the famed Mullova coolness something that I've imposed on her, simply to fit the popular preconception of her personality? Maybe. When talking to people who have worked regularly with her, a different picture certainly emerges. Sir Neville Marriner, for example, who has conducted many of her performances and recordings, explains to me, "Working with Mullova is quite revelatory vis-à-vis her temperament. Certainly as a social animal she's at first reserved and somewhat uncommunicative, but she displays a wicked sense of humor when she can relax.

"With the violin in her hand," he adds, "she's a technically assured executant with mature musical convictions. Perhaps the most satisfying performance I've shared with her was the one of the Berg Concerto. It's a work in which she reveals her temperamental secrets most comprehensively. She's a fascinating artist." So perhaps the simple answer to Mullova's reticence is that she takes her career, including the occasional interview, very seriously indeed. Another possibility is that she's capable of great warmth—artistic and personal—but that she's selective about who's shown it.

Costa Pilavachi's experience of her seems to bear this out. "It's difficult for me to agree with the suggestion that she's aloof and cold," he says. "She isn't really like that at all. And I wouldn't call her difficult by any stretch of the imagination, except that she has extremely high standards. She's very precise in terms of what she wants and how she wants it. Which isn't a problem; I mean, we've never had a disagreement about how many recording sessions to have, what edits to make, or anything like that.

"She's incredibly bright. She's quite highly strung. And her main attraction, apart from being a great musician, is that she's a person of immense curiosity. She's always exploring new music, wines, food, in fact life in general. She's also very bold and has a sense of adventure, which makes her exciting to be with."

Conductor Esa-Pekka Salonen offers another explanation of Mullova's image: "People can mistake clarity of phrasing for aloofness.

Recordings

Bach: Violin Sonatas and Partitas (Philips 434075-2).

Brahms: Violin Concerto. Berlin Philharmonic Orchestra, Claudio Abbado, cond. (Uni/Philips 438998-2).

Brahms: Violin Sonatas. With Piotr Anderszewski, piano (Philips Classics 446709-2).

Brahms: Piano Trio No. 1; Beethoven: Piano Trio No. 6. With André Previn, piano; Heinrich Schiff, cello (Philips 442123-2).

Debussy: Violin Sonata; Janáček: Violin Sonata; Prokofiev: Violin Sonata No. 1. With Piotr Anderszewski, piano (Philips 446091-2).

Mendelssohn: Violin and Strings Concerto; Violin Concerto, Op. 64. Academy of St. Martin in the Fields, Sir Neville Marriner, cond. (Philips 432077-2).

Sibelius: Violin Concerto; Tchaikovsky: Violin Concerto. Boston Symphony Orchestra, Seiji Ozawa, cond. (Philips 416821-2; 416821-5).

Stravinsky: Violin Concerto; Bartók: Violin Concerto. Los Angeles Philharmonic, Esa-Pekka Salonen, cond. (Uni/Philips 456542).

Tchaikovsky at Tea Time. Quartet for Strings No. 1 in D Major, Op. 1; Swan Lake, Op. 20; Concerto for Violin in D, Op. 35; Sleeping Beauty, Op. 66; Nutcracker Suite, Op. 71a; Variations for Cello and Orchestra on a Rococo Theme, Op. 3; Serenade for Strings in C Major, Op. 48; Trio for Piano and Strings in A Minor, Op. 50; Concerto for Piano No. 1 in B Flat Minor, Op. 23. Various orchestras and conductors (Uni/Philips 454498).

She doesn't move around much or jump up and down when she's performing; and because our culture is based so much on exterior appearances, these are often confused with the real substance of a person. If people aren't smart enough to work out what's real expression, then this confusion will probably still arise.

"She could have had a very flashy, superficial career based on the rather romantic story of the pretty girl who defected. But she's too good a musician to settle for that. She just goes for the core of the music, and I like that very direct approach. But she's also a very warm human being who enjoys life tremendously. If you actually listen to the sounds she makes, it's clear that she's a person of considerable emotional depth."

One of the most interesting aspects of her playing is the extent to which it has been influenced by the "early" or "authentic" music movement. She's clearly not a period-music performer, I suggest to her, yet she seems to play in a very Classical style. "Have you heard our recording [with her own chamber ensemble] of the Bach Concertos?" she asks. "We don't use period instruments, but you can probably feel the influence of authentic performance there. I think that the most important thing is *how* you play the music. The instrument matters sometimes, but not really very much. You can play Bach on any instrument. You can sing it or play it on the guitar and still be authentic.

"I like the period-instrument sound, and I enjoy listening to the *St. Matthew Passion* played on period instruments. The Beethoven symphonies, too. John Eliot Gardiner is one of my favorite musicians, and our music making together has influenced the way I play Bach and Mozart. In fact, I'm going through a big change in playing Mozart at the moment—I use gut strings for Mozart now. The sound has to be purer and absolutely clean, because sometimes you can distort it with gut strings and then it becomes ugly. The phrasing is different too: much more like speaking, a conversation. I can't stand listening to a romantic performance, with lots of vibrato, of pieces from the last century. Though of course Brahms is different."

This suggests that her repertoire is changing. One of her earliest recordings was of Paganini and Vieuxtemps concertos, and I tell her I don't really associate her with those composers now. "No, I don't play those any more. I find that kind of music less interesting. It's not so deep, and there's music that's much richer. Bach remains probably the greatest composer who ever lived, but his solo music, in particular, is technically very difficult. You have to understand the style it should be played in. I also like to play the Beethoven Concerto, and music of this century—Shostakovich, Stravinsky, and Bartók, for example." Music with a certain toughness, I venture. "Not only," returns Mullova. "There's also a lot of softness. I like a mixture."

I ask about her chamber group, the Mullova Ensemble, which she founded in 1994. "The group was formed for the recording of the Bach Concertos," she explains, "because our idea was to record them with an accompaniment of just seven instruments. So I invited some players, we did some tours in Italy, Germany, and the Netherlands, and then we recorded these Bach concertos in July 1995."

Regular contact with a small group of players like this can presumably help to combat the loneliness of a solo performer's career, I suggest. "Yes. As you say, it's different from touring alone. Traveling from one place to another, being in great company and a great atmosphere, with lots of jokes . . . and doing this not for money or for your career, but just for the pleasure of playing beautiful music together and learning from each other. The members of the Ensemble can't necessarily be big soloists, but they're really great musicians and I've learned a lot from them.

"The big project is to play and record the Mozart concertos on gut strings with the Orchestra of the Age of Enlightenment," she continues. "It will be like playing on a different instrument, and so I have to learn this instrument very well."

Recordings with Philips will also continue, and after 13 years with the company she's firmly established as one of its brightest stars. "She can now be considered at the peak of her powers," boasts Pilavachi, "and she's increasingly being recognized as a major international artist. The only other violinist we're committed to right now is Leila Josefowicz [see profile starting on page 15], but she's 20 years old and at the very beginning of her career. Obviously, every violinist is going to overlap with another, because the repertoire isn't endless, but Leila and Vika are very, very different."

Meanwhile, Mullova remains cautious about which works she takes into the studio. "So far," she explains, "Philips have agreed to record whatever I wanted, because I was myself trying not to develop my recording career too much. I've taken things slowly, and in 15 years I haven't recorded a lot. I'd rather wait. What's the point of doing an unsatisfactory recording and then wanting to do it again? You're never satisfied, of course, and you always change, but I was very lucky with my Bach recording. Just when I was about to record those Partitas, I realized that I didn't really know what I wanted to do with them. Philips were very good to me and agreed not to release the recording, and a year later, after I'd started listening to period instruments, they allowed me to record them again. But I hope not to repeat that kind of mistake, which is why I take time."

She says that she doesn't know when she'll record her beloved Beethoven Concerto. "It's just a mystery, that work. There isn't one recording of it that I like. This doesn't mean that I know how to play it myself. I'm trying hard to do it, but it's very, very difficult."

The Beethoven Concerto is certainly a familiar piece; a mark of its greatness, perhaps, is that it can be interpreted in so many ways. "There are lots of different ways to play this piece, but unfortunately it's interpreted in only one way—very romantic," she says. "It's not a true Romantic piece, it's a Classical piece. The danger is to go the other way and make it too dry. It's possible to play it on gut strings, but again, it's not easy, because everybody knows the wonderful sound of the Concerto on normal strings. So it's all about interpretation and phrasing."

For a musician of such serious intent, Mullova seems to place great emphasis on the way she presents herself visually in her often highly stylized CD portraits. Does she accept the recording industry's commodification of her as a performer, without fear that the packaging of a CD might be considered more important than its content? "In some cases it might," she answers, "but I don't really want to go into that area. Anyway, both are important, and it's nice when you have a good cover. Philips don't choose my photos, I do, and sometimes I make mistakes. But I think my covers are getting better."

She shows me her new CD of the Bartók Second and Stravinsky Concertos, pointing out how Philips has dispensed with the trademark dark red band that's usually incorporated into their booklet designs. "I'm very happy about that because the red disturbs the color of the picture," she says. "They've presented it really well. Look, there are lots of nice photos in it."

Mullova has succeeded in creating a solo career as well as a family.

Once again, I'm struck by the difference between the fragile and distracted-looking girl in the photographs and the quietly powerful woman sitting next to me. As our conversation draws to a close, I realize why she's so intriguing: she has the magnetism of someone who gives away sufficiently little of herself to always leave you hungry for more. Ultimately, of course, the issue of how reserved she is as a person has little importance; what matters is that, in Esa-Pekka Salonen's words, "she's one of the great violinists of today." But I do hope she won't feel that I've simply written more silly things about her.

Mark Kaplan

The American violinist Mark Kaplan has maintained flourishing careers in both the U.S. and Europe for more than two decades. He has performed with such orchestras as the New York and Los Angeles Philharmonics, the Cleveland and Philadelphia Orchestras, and the Chicago and National Symphony Orchestras. He has collaborated with renowned conductors including Eugene Ormandy, Kurt Masur, Charles Dutoit, Simon Rattle, and Esa-Pekka Salonen.

Kaplan also dedicates much of his time to the Golub-Kaplan-Carr trio. In the following interview, which appeared in Strings *magazine in December 1996, he discusses his career as a soloist, his dedication to chamber music, and his views on the future of classical music and musicians.*

Versatile Virtuoso

Edith Eisler

Mark Kaplan is one of those rare virtuosos who is also an extraordinarily versatile musician. His repertoire ranges from Baroque to contemporary and he is equally at home in concertos, recitals, and chamber music, both on the stage and on record. He plays with leading orchestras here and abroad, and he is also a member of the Golub-Kaplan-Carr Trio. His technique is dazzling but he uses it only in the service of the music, never for its own sake. His tone is beautiful and nuanced; he has the virtuoso's brilliance and flair without the self-indulgence. Playing with style, character, and expressiveness, he can turn bravura pieces into music.

Kaplan's musical upbringing was serious but, by his own account, did not interfere with a normal childhood. "I wasn't a child prodigy—I didn't play with the New York Philharmonic at the age of 12," he says. "I did little concerts appropriate to a child; I must have been 15 or 16 when I first played with a major orchestra, the Baltimore.

"I entered three competitions in the early 1970s, and I won the first, in Oakland, California. I didn't win the second, the Paganini Competition [in Genoa, Italy], but I did meet Joseph Szigeti, who was on the jury and whom I admired enormously. He was not in good health, and, in fact, he died soon afterward. But he summoned me to his bedside and talked to me for a long time about violin playing, because my performance had interested him. At the third, the 1973 Leventritt Competition in New York, there was no winner, but they gave me

something called an 'award of special distinction,' meant as a prize for the best contestant. They also helped me get some concerts for a while. But I think the most important thing about competitions is that you meet lots of people with similar interests. All this was a long time ago, but some of them are still very close friends of mine."

Alex Irvin

Kaplan is an extraordinarily versatile musician.

Describing his formative years, Kaplan says, "My native town of Syracuse, New York, was known, violinistically speaking, as the home of Louis Krasner [longtime violin and chamber-music teacher at the University of Syracuse]. I didn't study with him, but I knew him quite well, as well as his wife, Adrienne. They had an aura of another world about them; that was very interesting for me to have in my musical life. I also played quartets with them a few times when I was very young."

Kaplan was five or six when he started lessons with Carl Silfer, the associate concertmaster of the Syracuse Symphony Orchestra, who got him very excited and enthusiastic about the violin and, when he was about nine, sent him to New York to play for the famous pedagogues Ivan Galamian and Dorothy DeLay, who were working together then.

"Galamian was a very austere person, thoroughly intimidating for a kid that age," Kaplan remembers. "He didn't say hello, he just pointed to a worn-down spot on the carpet and said, 'Stand there and play me a C-major scale.' He kept telling me to play it faster, and finally he said, 'Now as fast as you can.' So I said, 'That was as fast as I can!' By contrast, Dorothy DeLay was warm and sweet and made me feel so happy and comfortable that, instead of working with both of them, I wanted to study only with her."

Kaplan recalls his time at the Juilliard School with humor and affection. "DeLay was a fantastic teacher with a genius for organizing violinistic knowledge. I came to her without a proper grasp of what I was doing technically, and she taught me everything I know. I worked with her until I graduated from Juilliard; I must have been 21 or 22. That's a long time, especially nowadays, when many people go from one teacher to another. But it was important for me to have somebody to guide my development over a long period, and she was extraordinary for that. I also went to Galamian's summer school at Meadowmount for five years and had a wonderful time; I still studied with DeLay, but I got to know Galamian well enough not to be scared of him any more.'"

DeLay concentrated on the concerto repertoire, so Kaplan studied sonatas with Felix Galimir, the renowned Viennese chamber musician and coach, whom Kaplan describes as "a delightful, wonderfully witty man. I remember playing with a pianist who had a rather percussive sound; at one point, Galimir got very excited and said to him, 'This note is so special, you must play it with a touch of mink!' The pianist gave him a puzzled look and tried it countless times, and when it finally sounded slightly better, Galimir said, 'Well, that was cheap mink, but it was mink a little bit!'"

Kaplan had the first of many European tours in 1976, the year he graduated from Juilliard, and has continued his solo career in both Europe and the U.S. He has performed some relatively new or unfamiliar concertos, such as the Penderecki and the Elliott Carter Concertos, and often combines concerts with other local musical activities. "I'm very much interested in teaching," he says. "I've done master classes in music schools and also conducted longer courses concentrating, for example, on unaccompanied Bach, which I often perform in concert."

Kaplan also started a prolific recording career that displays the versatility of his style. On a disc with the London Symphony under Mitch Miller, Paganini's Violin Concerto No. 1 becomes an Italian opera, Wieniawski's Concerto No. 2 a romantic drama. Another superb disc is all Sarasate—he seems to like concentrating on a single composer— with pianist Bruno Canino. This may seem like a lot of Sarasate, but the pieces are so varied, the playing so charming and idiomatic, that there is no danger of monotony. "I had a lot of fun making that record," Kaplan comments. "The music is wonderful, in its own way; I spent a lot of time listening to all the old records, including Sarasate's own. He was a most elegant player, with a style like quicksilver."

Also with Canino, there is an all-Bartók disc, which includes both Rhapsodies ("He wrote them first with piano and then orchestrated them, but I think both versions were equally authentic for him") and the Solo Sonata, a famously—and infamously—difficult work in a masterly performance. More recently, he recorded the second Bartók Concerto and the second Dohnányi Concerto, which had never been recorded before, with the Orchestra of Barcelona under Foster, and the Viotti Concertos Nos. 4, 22, and 24 with the Chamber Orchestra of Padua under David Golub.

Kaplan writes his own liner notes, which are both informative and entertaining; his adventurous, inquisitive mind leads him to discover not only unfamiliar music but also unknown facts about familiar music. His Schumann disc features three sonatas; at least half of the third is completely unknown. He explains, "Schumann took his two movements from the 'F-A-E' Sonata, which he had written for [Joseph] Joachim together with Albert Dietrich and Brahms, and added two

What He Plays

Mark Kaplan's violin is an Antonio Stradivari made in 1685, which he thinks of as "the Bach year," since it was the year of the composer's birth. "It is called 'The Marquis,'" Kaplan says of his instrument, "because it once belonged to the family of the Marchese of Spinola in Italy. It was lost for a while, then a violinist in a touring American orchestra picked it up in Italy in the 1970s for the ridiculous sum of $5,000 and sold it to a dealer in London, from whom I bought it 12 years ago." His bow, which he has on loan, is a François Tourte; his strings are Pirastro Olives, except the E, which is a Hill.

Alex Irvin

more. Along with other pieces he wrote just before his suicide attempt, his wife Clara hid them away, and the Sonata was not published until 1956. I like it and think it's well worth playing."

The pianist on that record is Anton Kuerti, who was Kaplan's partner the very first time I heard him, in a sonata recital at New York's 92nd Street YMHA a number of years ago. When I tell him that I still remember the performance of the Schubert *Fantasie*, he smiles. "Thank you! Anton is a wonderful pianist. I met him at the Santa Fe Chamber Music Festival; he invited me to a Schubert festival he was doing in Toronto. He is also a great Schumann player, so I immediately thought of him for this Schumann recording. We never established a regular duo, but we've played together a lot over the years."

David Golub is the pianist of the Golub-Kaplan-Carr Trio, which Kaplan cofounded in 1982, when he had already begun to play professionally in chamber-music festivals. I asked him how the group began and developed. "David and I were at Juilliard at the same time; we got to know each other and sometimes played together," Kaplan explains. "The first thing we did in public was the Alban Berg *Kammerkonzert*, and then we started assembling groups for chamber music. We once invited [cellist] Colin Carr, who had just won the Naumburg Competition, to read some trios; it sounded awfully good, so we decided we should really give some concerts. The trio has been playing together ever since."

"Playing in public has both the advantage and the disadvantage that you can only do it once."

Kaplan's home is in New Jersey; Golub lives in Milan, Italy (although he is also a member of the Chamber Music Society of Lincoln Center); and Carr is based in Boston. Living in different cities, how do the trio members manage rehearsals?

"We get together before a tour, but we don't have a regular rehearsal schedule," Kaplan says. "One of the purposes of forming the trio was to explore the literature, so at the beginning we just learned and performed an enormous amount of music very quickly. Now that we're 'old and wise,' we try to limit the number of pieces we do in a season, though we add some new things every year, including some recently written works. In February, at the Chamber Music Society of Lincoln Center, for example, we played a trio by the English composer Nicholas Maw; he wrote it about five years ago, and it's a great piece.

"One piece we play a lot is the Beethoven Triple Concerto," Kaplan continues. "Many people regard it as one of Beethoven's lesser works, but I believe we bring something special to it that proves them wrong. (I feel I can boast about the trio, because I'm only a third of it.) When the piece is performed by three soloists, even very good ones, it often becomes fragmented, because they are all just focusing on their own parts, while a full-time trio doesn't always sound soloistic enough. Our group tries to capitalize on both worlds by playing like individual soloists and still reacting to the orchestra and conductor like a single unit. That requires an extraordinary level of communication between us, a subtle realization of who's leading and whom the conductor must follow at any given moment."

Ales Irvin

I bring up a question long on my mind. "The first time I heard your group, you played the Schubert E Flat Trio. The program said you were restoring some prepublication cuts, and a few passages did seem new to me. What's the story about that?"

"It's very interesting," Kaplan answers. "Schubert himself made some cuts in the last movement, two sections totaling about 100 bars in the development. But the new urtext editions include them. It was our record company that suggested we play the cut measures—record companies like doing something different. We thought that if Schubert cut them, he probably knew what he was doing; but we learned them,

"There is a popular illusion that art, like virtue, is its own reward."

and we recorded both versions. And we found that when we first put in those 100 measures, we didn't think it worked at all, but once we'd learned them, we felt something was missing when we left them out. And it's fascinating, because one of those sections combines the cello solo from the slow movement with the repeated-note theme of the finale. So now we always play it entirely uncut.

"Basically, I don't believe in cuts; they mutilate the music. We just released a recording of the Tchaikovsky Trio on which we make no cuts at all, though I know most people do in the Variations, or they leave out the Fugue because they say it's not well written. In a sense, that's true—nobody wrote fugues like Bach, not even Beethoven. But you have to respect the composer; the music is what it is."

One of my favorites among the trio's recordings is *French Piano Trios*, which sounds particularly beautiful and features works by Debussy, Saint-Saëns, and Fauré. I ask about the problems of recording a trio, where not only the sound of the individual instruments, but their balance, has to be faithfully reproduced.

"It's difficult, but by this time we know each other well enough to make it work. With each record, we get more experience and refine things a bit more; the French one is among the most recent, and maybe that's why it sounds best."

How does making a recording compare to playing in public?

"It's entirely different," Kaplan says. "Playing in public has both the advantage and the disadvantage that you can only do it once, which means that you can take all your energy and concentrate it into a very short period of time. The result is usually that you have an extra dimension in a live performance that you lack on a recording. And of course there is the element of interaction with the audience. The more you perform, the more you appreciate that, and the more you also learn to communicate, which is really what it's all about. When I started making records, I wanted them to sound like concerts. And in a sense I still do, but now I realize that they're not concerts, and I think that enables me to relax and actually make better records.

"I also learned that if you have a good producer, you should trust him or her. If you try to be your own producer, to listen and decide, 'Is this what I want or was it better yesterday?' that's too much. That's the producer's responsibility. It's hard enough to keep up the intensity, the emotional connectedness to the music, for seven hours today and seven more tomorrow. When I'm making a record, I have so much invested in it psychologically that I find I can't listen to it afterward for a long time—and frankly, I don't listen to my own records a lot. Not long ago, I happened to hear our Brahms trios on the radio; we'd made the record five years before and changed so many things that, for a while, I wasn't sure I recognized it."

I ask him what he thinks the future holds for recordings.

"The industry did something very smart: it created CDs and then created a market for them," he answers. "But now, that market is saturated. In the old days, you had a record, it got scratchy, you replaced it; or, when stereo records came out, they sounded significantly better than mono, so you bought some. On compact discs, the sound is so good that, for the ordinary listener, the differences between the various qualities of technology are minimal. The discs last forever, but they stay in the catalog and pile up, so the companies have to find ways to sell them, and increasingly the promotion focuses on personalities and cult figures and has nothing to do with music. I think the record industry is headed for a very difficult time."

However, it is on the subject of the state of classical music in general that Kaplan holds the strongest opinions and expresses them the most eloquently. "There is a real crisis in classical music in the United States today," he says. "It may not be as apparent in New York as in the rest of America, but it's a very serious situation. When I was growing up in Syracuse, we had three recital series. I heard all the great players: [Nathan] Milstein, [David] Oistrakh, [pianist Arthur] Rubinstein, [pianist Sviatoslav] Richter. . . . Now all those series are gone, orchestras are closing down, and wherever you go, people are complaining that there's not enough audience, especially young audience.

"The reason is not hard to find. When I was a kid, elementary schools had orchestras and you could study any instrument. Hardly any of the students became musicians, but they did become lovers of classical

Recordings

Bartók: *Violin Concerto No. 2; Dohnányi: Violin Concerto No. 2. Barcelona Symphony Orchestra, Lawrence Foster, cond. (Koch International Classics KIC 7387).*

Bartók: *Violin Works. With Bruno Canino (Arabesque 6649).*

Brahms: *Horn Trio; Piano Trio No. 1. David Jolley, horn; David Golub, piano; Colin Carr, cello (Arabesque Z 6607).*

Brahms: *Piano Trios Nos. 2 and 3. With David Golub, piano; Colin Carr, cello (Arabesque Z 6608).*

Dvořák: *Complete Piano Trios. With David Golub, piano; Colin Carr, cello (Arabesque 6726).*

Dvořák: *Czech Suite; Notturno; Serenade. Padova Chamber Orchestra, David Golub, cond. (Arabesque ARA 6697).*

French Piano Trios: *Works by Saint-Saëns, Debussy, and others. With David Golub, piano; Colin Carr, cello (Arabesque 6643).*

Mendelssohn: *Piano Trios Nos. 1 and 2. With David Golub, piano; Colin Carr, cello (Arabesque Z 6599).*

Sarasate: *Violin and Piano Music. With Bruno Canino, piano (Arabesque Z 6614).*

Schubert: *Piano Nocturne; Piano Trios No. 1 and 2. With David Golub, piano; Colin Carr, cello (Arabesque 2-Z 6580-2).*

Schubert: *Violin Rondo, D. 895; Violin Sonatinas. With David Golub, piano (Arabesque ARA 6636).*

Schuman: *Violin Sonatas Nos. 1, 2, and 3. With Anton Kuerti, piano (Arabesque ARA 6662).*

Smetana and Tchaikovsky: *Piano Trios. With David Golub, piano; Colin Carr, cello (Arabesque Z 6661).*

Viotti: *Violin Concertos Nos. 4, 22, and 24. Padova Chamber Orchestra, David Golub, cond. (Arabesque ARA 6691).*

music and members of future audiences. Most of these public-school programs were cut and a whole generation has grown up thinking that classical music is weird, for eggheads. So all the rather desperate attempts to create audiences, like community outreach programs, face an uphill battle. And now there is this big uproar in Congress about the National Endowment, supposedly because a few projects it supported were distasteful to some people. But why doesn't anyone speak up and say, if a governmental or private agency that distributes money spends maybe 5 percent on complete trash, but has an efficiency rate of 95 percent, wouldn't you think it's doing fabulously? That's the real point.

"Now here's my suggestion," he continues. "I live in New Jersey, and we have a system that lets you donate a small sum to an environmental or wildlife fund by putting it on your tax form. It's voluntary and lots of people do it. Why can't we have something like that on the federal tax form to support the arts? It would be totally democratic, nobody would have to do it unless they wanted to, and, as with any charitable donation, they'd get a tax deduction. If even a small percentage of people gave $10, it would come to a lot more than the whole NEA budget, which is only a drop in the bucket anyway. Some people say the private sector should step in—that instead of government support, there should be corporate sponsorship. That's fine, but a little whimsical: in bad times, even the most generous corporations come under pressure and shouldn't feel responsible for keeping the arts alive. It was different when the church and the aristocracy patronized the arts; they were pretty stable institutions that could be counted on. And the art they helped to create was not elitist; a lot of it was available to everybody."

How will musicians weather these adversities? Kaplan sighs. "Well, it won't be easy. There is a popular illusion that art, like virtue, is its own reward, so it's all right to let artists starve. Musicians don't expect to get rich, but they do have to live. And what's more, virtue can be practiced silently, but art demands to be communicated."

Korean violinist Chee-Yun began performing early: she won the Grand Prize of the Korean Times Competition at age eight. Her teacher in Korea was Nam Yun Kim; she came to New York (where she is currently based) in 1983, at age 13, to study at the Juilliard School. There she worked with the noted teacher Dorothy DeLay as well as with Hyo Kang and the renowned chamber musician Felix Galimir.

She has won numerous awards, including the 1989 Young Concert Artists International Auditions, the 1990 Avery Fisher Career Grant, and the 1993 Nan Pa award of South Korea, the country's highest musical honor. She has performed as a soloist with the Philadelphia Orchestra, the National Symphony, the San Francisco Symphony, and the Cincinnati Symphony, and she tours as a chamber-music artist with the Spoleto Festival U.S.

This interview took place in June 2000, after her performance of Beethoven's "Archduke" Trio with cellist Andrés Díaz and pianist Stephen Prutsman at the venerable Dock Street Theatre, as part of the Spoleto Festival in Charleston, South Carolina.

The Exuberant Professional

Robert Moon

Chee-Yun rushes to shake my hand with the exuberance of a young musician under the influence of playing publicly, for the first time, one of the great masterpieces of chamber music: Beethoven's Piano Trio No. 7 in B Flat the "Archduke." She immediately replays the performance in words.

"Sometimes when you're playing you're thinking, 'This is so tough,' and you're really concentrating on the detail . . . but today there were moments when I was getting goosebumps. In the slow movement I was actually praying, it was so spiritual. It was a moment when I realized that this is why we do what we do," she says enthusiastically. "We were all so nervous, saying we have to do this masterpiece justice. Then Steve [Prutsman] said, 'How many times do we get to play great music for the first time?' My attitude changed, and I realized I would give it my best, just play the notes and let the music flow like butter."

Beneath this youthful and effervescent personality lies a musician who speaks frankly about the rigors of the life of a professional violinist. "Traveling is so hard," she acknowledges. "Oh, I want to take weekends off, go out with my friends—but then, experiences like playing the 'Archduke' make it all worthwhile."

Two weeks later, she plays Lou Harrison's Suite for Violin with American Gamelan in San Francisco's Davies Hall, and there it is clear that the effort of her early years has created a musician with not only technique—that of a virtuoso, in fact—but also with a rich, vibrant tone and a presence to match. How does a prodigy become a mature musician?

You started playing at age six. How did you get started?

My mother was a modern woman: she really wanted to learn how to play the piano and be a piano teacher, rather than assume the traditional role of being a good cook and a good wife. My older brother was born first, and, like most Asian men, he got most of the attention. When my mother then had two girls, she started giving them music lessons. I was the fourth child and became a tomboy, playing with my older brother. And my long hair actually is a rebellion against my mom, who was constantly chopping it off to prevent me from playing with it!

But I wanted to be like my sisters, and my older sister was a piano player, a little prodigy. She was really good and getting all the attention. So I started playing the piano at age four or five so I could get some attention, too. I loved the sound of the piano and started learning more than my teacher asked of me. Playing the piano was easy and fun for me.

But then my mother thought that my eyes were getting crossed from playing the piano. She had me stop the lessons, so I looked for something else to do. My other sister was playing the violin, but she hated it—she wanted to become a ballerina. So I started playing the violin.

By the time I was seven years old I was taking lessons, but I wasn't very motivated and practiced little. My mom wanted me to stop, but my teacher objected, saying that there was something in my playing that would merit continuing. My mom suggested that I enter a competition as a way to motivate me to practice. So at age eight, I entered the Korean Times Competition as an unknown, and I won it. I had never played on stage before, and I instantly fell in love with it!

Winning that competition convinced me that I was good enough to be a professional violinist. I went to study with a Korean professor who was studying with Ivan Galamian and I decided I was going next to Juilliard. When I got there, I was a little frog in the ocean. Midori was there and was having a career after three years. I played in a quartet with her (all of us were 12 or 13 years old—she played the viola) and I remember we played the first movement of the Dvořák "American" Quartet for a birthday party and earned $50. That was big money for me!

Has it been hard for you to practice regularly?

Practice today for me is much more fun than it used to be. I went through a period when I wished I could go to sleep with the music in my head and wake up having it all memorized. I went through a lazy period where I wanted to go to movies and go out with boys, driving my mom and dad crazy. I would go through periods where I just wanted to quit playing the violin. My parents would say, "Just go ahead, we can sell your violin and buy a nice car with the money." And then I would go back to it.

Nancy Ellison

What kept me going was having a great teacher, Miss [Dorothy] DeLay. She was consistently supportive and encouraging. When I went through a real teenage crisis—losing a boyfriend—I would go to my lesson, my eyes welling up with tears. She would say, "Come here, sit next to me, listen and talk to me." I felt she really cared about me as a person, not just as a violinist. When I came to the States, there were so many great players. Who was going to notice me—especially why Miss DeLay? She'd heard this work played by [Itzhak] Perlman, Nadja Salerno-Sonnenberg, Midori, all of them a thousand times better than me. How was I going to prove myself? And I didn't speak English! I was just another one of those little kids.

"I started playing piano at age four or five so I could get some attention."

So I worked so hard for every lesson, like getting ready for a performance. When I went through those years of personal crises, she helped me survive them. I even left home for three days. My mom begged me to come home and my dad said, "Don't come home, I'm going to disown you!" And then Miss DeLay just drove me home—how about that! And she explained to my dad that what I was going through was temporary, just part of being a teenager.

Since you've been out of school, about how many concerts do you play in a year?

I play between 50 and 60 orchestral dates a year. I play a lot of concertos, but I also tour with a group of five of us who play chamber music—[pianist] Steve Prutsman, [cellist] Andrés Diaz, [pianist and artistic director for Spoleto's chamber music concerts] Charles Wadsworth, [clarinetist] Todd Palmer, and me—under the name of Spoleto USA. We do two different tours a year, playing ten to 12 concerts on each tour. During the summer I play several festivals. This summer I'm going to the Bravo! Vail Valley Music Festival in Colorado, to Spoleto in South Carolina, and to the La Jolla Summerfest in California. I love going to festivals, and Spoleto was my first one, back in 1993. Playing chamber music at the summer festivals has played a significant role in my maturation as a musician.

What She Plays

Chee-Yun plays a 1669 Francesco Ruggieri violin, about which she speaks enthusiastically. "Ruggieri was one of Niccolò Amati's first known disciples. This is one of the most perfect specimens in terms of its condition: no scratches, no evidence of any damage. It has extraordinarily beautiful wood. It was virtually a brand-new instrument when I bought it; to my knowledge, there have been no previous violinists who have owned it.

"The sound was very small when I got it. Miss DeLay told me that Ruggieri's violins were better chamber-music instruments, but not the best for playing concertos. The instrument has a great, sweet quality, but it lacks volume. But I told her I wasn't interested in a big sound; I was more concerned about having a sweet, good sound, and that I felt I often played too loudly anyway.

"I played this violin for [DeLay] a year later, and she wondered if it was the same violin. It sounded just right for me. Orchestra members often comment on how incredibly beautiful this instrument sounds."

Chee-Yun uses an F.N. Voirin bow, made between 1870 and 1875, and Thomastik Dominant strings.

Recordings

French Violin Sonatas. *Fauré: Violin Sonata No. 1 in A Major, Op. 13; Debussy: Violin Sonata; Saint-Saëns: Violin Sonata No. 1 in D Major, Op. 75. With Akira Eguchi, piano* (Denon CO-75625).

Lalo: Symphonie Espagnole, Op. 21; Saint-Saëns: Violin Concerto No. 3 in B Minor, Op. 61. London Philharmonic Orchestra, Jesus Lopez-Cobos, cond. (Denon CO 18017).

Mendelssohn: Violin Concerto in E Minor, Op. 64; Vieuxtemps: Violin Concerto No. 5 in A Major, Op. 37. London Philharmonic Orchestra, Jesus Lopez-Cobos, cond. (Denon CO 78913).

Penderecki: Second Violin Concerto (forthcoming).

Szymanowski: Sonata for Violin and Piano in D Minor, Op. 9; Franck: Sonata for Violin and Piano in A Major. With Akira Eguchi, piano (Denon CO 78954).

Vocalise: *Violin Show Pieces: Works by Elgar, Rimsky-Korsakov, Rachmaninov, Szymanowski, Bernstein, Khachaturian, Suk, Fauré, Massenet, Sarasate. With Akira Eguchi, piano* (Denon CO 75118).

Why is chamber music so attractive to you?

I started playing chamber music a lot in 1990, after I went to the Marlboro Music Festival [in Vermont]. Chamber music is great because you get to work with high-caliber musicians who are willing to share their knowledge and experience with you. I love getting constructive criticism and feedback in a rehearsal. I sit at the rehearsal and I ask my colleagues, "How is this?" I listen to their answers and I try them out. I might have my own ideas, but I'm curious to know what they're thinking first. To play on stage with them is great fun—the spontaneous give-and-take that happens is really special. Chamber music has helped me play concertos because I listen to the orchestra more closely now.

Nancy Ellison

What is it like playing a concerto for an orchestra for the first time?

When I meet the orchestra, I want to be with them, rather than be a soloist apart from them. They don't know you, and you know they're saying, "Oh, another Asian violinist, all fingers but very doubtful as a musician." And that's fine, and I'm there to prove them wrong!

> "When I meet the orchestra, I want to be with them, rather than be a soloist apart from them."

Soloists often need to lead the orchestra when playing a concerto, but sometimes it's actually better to follow the conductor and listen carefully to what's going on in the orchestra rather than just play your solo part. I want to be part of the orchestra. I want to be able to hear the strings and the winds just as much as the conductor does. I know the score, I know what's going on, and I want to make it all work. Orchestra musicians really appreciate that. And then they come up to me afterward, and say, "Wow, you really make music. It was fun playing with you."

I want them to enjoy the experience as much as I do. How great it is that I get to play with all those musicians on stage, rather than trying to be in the spotlight as a soloist.

How many rehearsals do you have with the orchestra?

One or two at the most. It isn't enough, and when the conductor spends too much time on the other symphonic works on the program, it can get ugly. There usually isn't a piano rehearsal with the conductor—unless it's a new work, and then the conductors want to spend a lot of time with the soloist. If they know the work and have played it many times, then all the conductor usually wants is a run through.

What makes a good conductor, from your perspective?

Sensitivity, someone who is open to my ideas about interpretation, and someone with a willingness to allow spontaneous things to happen;

someone who exerts leadership, which means achieving rapport between me, as the soloist, and the orchestra. That's so important, because if you don't have rapport with the orchestra, they won't follow you. A lot of times it's a combination of musical and personal issues. The good conductors I work with know exactly what to say in rehearsals, when to say it, and how to say it. How often to stop and interrupt. The good conductors are well prepared; they have a plan and know how they want to work with this rehearsal. And of course it's easier to work with conductors who are familiar with me.

A conductor has to know a whole lot more about a piece than I do, because he's conducting the whole orchestra. So I go to him with the score and I ask him how this or that phrase works dynamically, how does it fit in, and should I come in at a higher volume level because the winds are playing, even though the score says piano, and so forth.

Of the concerts you do, in how many are you really playing in top form?

That's a good question. Often I feel like I'm not really playing as well as I can. Every time you go on stage, you're completely exposed. People

"Every time you go on stage, you're completely exposed."

expect you to play at this incredibly high level every time. There are days that I'm slightly off and don't play as well. People don't know that you might have a really bad flu one night, and that your head is so stuffed up that your hearing goes in and out. Then there are days where you really are on.

I was on tour with the San Francisco Symphony this spring and played the Mendelssohn Concerto seven times. In New Haven, Connecticut, it was very hot and humid, and a huge storm deluged the streets just before the concert. I felt really good on that day and I decided to go for it. And everything worked out. One of the factors that makes a difference is to decide to really go all out rather than hold back. If you worry too much or are insecure in your playing, it shows. It sounds as if you're scared, nothing is coming off your ideas, and you can't communicate. So, the more I decide to go for it, even though it might not always work, the better I become overall.

Do you play contemporary music as well?

I just finished recording the Penderecki Concerto No. 2 for Naxos. It's a great piece, and the more I play it the more I like it. And when I played with the California Symphony [in May 2000], I met the composer-in-residence, Kevin Putz. He gave me a CD of his works and I liked them a great deal. So I've commissioned him to write me a work for solo violin.

What role has recording played in the development of your career?

Artistically, recording forces you to prepare a piece even more meticulously than a performance. I consider myself a perfectionist. When I prepare for recordings, I'm really hard on myself. I hate to do a lot of takes, because when you do that the music becomes dead.

But when you listen to a recording that is perfect in every way, often you never want to listen to it again. It's so boring. I like recordings that feel like a live concert: you feel the drive, and the phrases go somewhere. That's how I prepared the Penderecki Concerto, which I played with Antoni Wit and the Polish National Radio Symphony. I was able to record the work in big chunks, and I told the producer that I was looking for excitement and the "live concert" feeling. I can't wait until the recording comes out, as I think it's one I will be really proud of.

Do you listen to your recordings?

Well, no. Although people say nice things about my past recordings, I just cringe at some of the details. I want to do them over again—do I ever! And it's been four years since I made my last recording [the Lalo *Symphonie espagnole* and the Saint-Saëns Violin Concerto No. 3, with the London Philharmonic Orchestra conducted by Jesús Lopez-Cobos]. I didn't do anything with Denon for a while because the producer I worked with left the company, but they rehired him, and they want to renew my contract.

What composers really move you?

I like melodic pieces. Tonal music. To tell you the truth, I wasn't crazy about Beethoven, though. I always thought I would wait awhile before playing the Beethoven Concerto, and I'm still going to wait several years until I play that piece. I'm going to go back and study it again, now that I've played the "Archduke" Trio. I've been to concerts where young violinists play the Beethoven Concerto—and then I heard Milstein play it at his last concert [on recording], and it was phenomenal. That kind of experience and depth is really needed, and I'm not ready to play it yet. The Brahms Concerto is also one I haven't played yet, but it is scheduled for next season [2000–01].

What violinists are your heroes?

All the contemporary violinists who are playing are heroes and heroines to me.

What about past violinists?

Michael Rabin [1936–72], Henryk Szeryng [1918–88]. Szeryng is so spiritual and spontaneous.

Are there any works you're dying to play that you haven't played?

The Barber Concerto is in my repertoire, but I haven't played it [publicly] yet. It is so beautiful. And I'm looking forward to playing the Brahms next year.

What kind of music do you listen to?

I listen to classical radio stations when I'm in the car. I love to listen to opera—Maria Callas was my favorite. She was a great actress and sang with such feeling. I've seen her videotapes, and the drama she infuses into her roles comes through in her recordings as well. I try to do that when I play. The stringed instruments are really closest to the human voice, and a lot of times in a piece I'm playing I'll try to sing, to imitate the most beautiful voices. The second movement of the "Archduke" Trio is an example.

Why are there so many great Asian musicians, especially string players?

The biggest reason is that, at least in my parents' generation, the mother always stayed home with their children to nurture and motivate them. I don't remember any students who were successful at Juilliard, whether they were from here or Korea, who did not have one parent who came with them to Juilliard. There are as many Asian piano players as string players, maybe not as many wind players. Right now the violin is probably more popular, but when I was a little girl, the piano was more common. Parents have such a strong influence on a child's character, and I think the mothers' full-time role has been the major reason there are so many Asian musicians today.

How have you grown musically in the last few years?

When I was a little girl I had confidence on stage, but it was show-off confidence. As I grew and got nervous before performing, insecurity set in and I started doubting myself. That lasted for several years.

Then, in the last five years, I began to drop the insecurity and decided to go all out in my playing. It's as if I had played the works millions of times and there was no hesitation. That meant that I started taking risks, and the music began to come alive on a more consistent basis. The risk-taking began to open my mind and then I began to think less of being scared. My intonation got so much better when I started taking risks, my phrasing became much more musical. It also has a lot to do with playing chamber music, taking music apart with chamber musicians and learning from them. I'm so grateful and lucky that Charles Wadsworth invited me to play chamber music, almost all of which I played for the first time.

Twenty-five years from now, what is the most important thing you hope you will have contributed to the music world?

I love young children. I hope I will be able to pass on my wisdom—when I have some! I see so many great young players now, and they're so advanced at such an early age. I'd like to share with them what it means to be a part of mankind, and to pass on what I've learned about classical music. I've taught a couple of students and it's been a great experience, and I've realized that *I've* learned so much by teaching.

And I would be pleased if people came to me and said, "Your playing spoke to me; I felt it." That would be the biggest compliment I could receive.

Christian Tetzlaff

By always taking the road less traveled, the German violinist Christian Tetzlaff has established himself as an extraordinary player with an extraordinary career. In an age when talented youngsters are pushed into performing earlier and earlier, he did not start practicing seriously until he was a teenager; and he has achieved worldwide recognition without having had to win a prestigious prize, usually considered the quickest path to success.

Tetzlaff's independence of mind is matched by a prodigious talent: he uses his masterful technique and flawlessly pure, beautiful tone—warm, intense, and austere rather than sweet or lush—to serve the music and express his highly intelligent, personal approach to it. The following is drawn from two interviews Tetzlaff gave to Strings *magazine, one in 1994 and one in 1997. When we spoke the second time, we decided to start by discussing Bach's six unaccompanied Sonatas and Partitas, to which Tetzlaff feels particularly close and which he was looking forward to playing frequently in 2000, during the worldwide celebrations of the 250th anniversary of Bach's death. His performance of the cycle at New York's Alice Tully Hall in April 2000 was indeed outstanding.*

Independent Thinker

Edith Eisler

Photo by Cylla Von Tiedemann

Christian Tetzlaff is that rare musical phenomenon, a virtuoso violinist who possesses not only a brilliant technique but also a brilliant mind. From the beginning of his musical studies, he worked out his own ideas, which gave him an independent, personal point of view; he talks about music in general, and about specific works in particular, with a combination of scholarly intellectual rigor, enthusiasm, and a sense of adventure.

Tetzlaff first came to international attention at the 1988 Berlin Festival when he was 22, with a performance of the notoriously difficult Schoenberg Concerto. He played it again at his American debut in Cleveland the same year, proving himself to be not only one of the best but one of the most adventurous and daring young violinists. The program he chose for his New York recital debut in 1993 reinforced that reputation: it consisted of unaccompanied works by Bach, Bartók, and Ysaÿe. Since then, he has appeared in New York in recitals, as well as at the Mostly Mozart Festivals of 1994 and 1998 in Mozart's Concertos Nos. 1 and 3, and at Carnegie Hall in the Mendelssohn Concerto on a 1997 coast-to-coast tour with the Deutsche Symphonie-Orchester Berlin under Vladimir Ashkenazy.

I remember when we talked in 1994, you told me that you had not yet performed the B-Minor Partita in concert, only on record.

Well, I have since then, many times, but I still think it is a shocker, a really terribly difficult piece; I play it with great fear and admiration. But the D-Minor Partita is wonderful to play.

Do you play them in chronological order?

Of course, that's how the story goes.

The story?

Yes, there is a very profound, religious story, and Bach supports it with many citations from chorales on the same themes. The three Sonatas are church sonatas in which he is commenting on the cycle of the church year: Christmas, Passion, and Easter. The G-Minor Sonata represents Christmas, with many quotes from Christmas chorales. The "Siciliano" is a typical pastoral, perhaps implying the shepherds in the field; the downward run at the end of the preceding Fugue might signify the descent of the Angels for the Annunciation. The A-Minor Sonata represents Christ and His Passion, it is focused on His person, again with many references to chorales of which He is the theme. And it is well known that the Fugue theme in the C-Major Sonata is based on the chorale *Veni, Creator Spiritus,* so that Sonata represents Pentecost, again with many references to chorales on that theme. The Fugue begins on a downward line to show that help descends from above; the inversion turns upward, but later turns back down again to indicate man's unworthiness. In that movement, Bach quotes from the preceding sonatas, going back to the very beginning of the whole set. But in the Partitas, Bach presents the earthly side of life, with its dancing, joyful quality.

But the D-Minor Partita is very dark, not life-affirming at all.

Yes, here the two sides collide. He wrote the Chaconne the year his wife died—it is a requiem for her; it has citations from many chorales that deal with death. There is a clear connection between the Chaconne and the movement that follows it, the Adagio of the C-Major Sonata: both have the same meter and dotted rhythm, and the tonality of the Adagio is so ambiguous that it might be a continuation of what came before. It doesn't settle into C major until the end of the movement, where it offers the first hopeful outlook into a major mode. Then the Fugue, like an apparition from Heaven, steps down as "help from above." In the C-Major Sonata, Bach is finding himself again after his anger and despair at his wife's death; it is a purification through religion.

So there certainly is a story here. One should really play all six pieces in one evening, but that would be just too much, so I do it in two. I get the four pieces in minor in the beginning, then the C-Major; the E-Major Partita is actually only a dance suite, but it's a confirmation of the hope generated in the C-Major Sonata: now we may enjoy life. I don't even make a break between the D-Minor and the C-Major, which is a challenge, but it makes a lot of sense.

Then there is another thing. You know that Bach was always manipulating numbers, as many people did at that time. They numbered the letters, and the corresponding musical notes, according to the alphabet: A=1, D=4, and so on. So the note-numbers in the first statement of the Chaconne theme add up to the year of his wife's death. That is why Bach sometimes repeats only the top note of the chord, sometimes the entire chord.

Tetzlaff possesses not only a brilliant technique but also a brilliant mind.

Really! I always thought he did that for the sonority.

Another example: the first bar of the D-minor Allemande adds up to the same number as his wife's complete name: Anna Barbara Bach. It works because the D in that bar is doubled and counts as eight.

I thought he did that for the voice leading: the upper D goes up the scale, the lower one down to the C-sharp.

Yes, that's another reason. Isn't it amazing how Bach handled all these complexities? He was an incredibly brilliant man. He also used the numbering tradition in his cantatas and *Passions,* and there one can verify the meaning of the numbers by the words that are being sung. For example, the words "And the curtain of the Temple was rent in twain" in the *St. Matthew Passion* are accompanied by the strings with a tremolo of 128 notes, to correspond to Psalm 128, which is being quoted.

He made a big differentiation between his "musica sacra" and "musica populare." In the sacred works, he sometimes wrote the music in the shape of a cross, and chose keys with a lot of sharps [the German word

What He Plays

When I first met Tetzlaff in 1994, he played on a Stradivari violin on loan, the "Cox Rothschild," made in 1713. In 1996, he still had the Strad, but he had also acquired a brand new violin made for him by Peter Greiner, who lives in Bonn. Since then, Tetzlaff has passed on that violin and another one made by Greiner in 1997 to other violinists; he now plays two Greiner violins made in 1999 that were modeled on a Guarneri del Gesù instrument.

Tetzlaff uses a Voirin bow, and he also has a contemporary bow by Benoit Rolland. He uses a new line of strings developed by Dominant. The company made custom G and E strings for him.

In 1997 I asked him about his first Greiner. Why did he feel he wanted a modern fiddle? "I suppose because I saw some of Mr. Greiner's violins," he said. "They were really outstanding, and I thought it would be fascinating to see whether it is possible to reach the level of a Guarneri or a Stradivari with a new instrument. When he started building the violin, he said, 'It will be difficult to match the sound of the Strad's D string,' and I thought, 'Well, he is quite ambitious to aim so high and think he can even come close.' But his confidence in himself proved to be completely justified. He concerns himself with every aspect of violin making: going through the woods, looking for the right trees, making sure they are the right age. And of course the aesthetics of an instrument are very important. That's why he copied my Strad—it's the perfect model—and why he keeps trying to match the depth, the golden brown color of the varnish. Even when he makes instruments that are entirely in his own style, he still aims for that kind of beauty."

Did it take long to play the violin in? "It was very good from the first day, but we are still making changes to the sound. Since we were able to work on the copy but not on the Strad, I think that gave the copy a chance to end up even better than the Strad. Modern instruments have the possibility to change more just because the wood is still alive. It takes a maker a long time to find the perfect balance, the best sound an instrument has to give. Playing Sibelius and Mendelssohn, I feel so much more comfortable on the Greiner; it has the easy strength, the darkness. With the Strad, not having the easy strength can be good for the character of the sound, and it certainly shows up in the piano and in the colors that are more malleable, more touching, in Mozart, for example. In some ways, I think you have to compromise in solo playing, because you must have incredible strength and that necessarily goes against some of the colors. I feel the Greiner combines both in a better way than the Strad at the moment."

I asked if he could use the Greiner for the big Romantic repertoire and the Strad for everything else. "I would have to start with one fiddle and change to the other. It would be quite easy," he replied.

This, however, is not the end of the story. When Tetzlaff returned to New York in 1998, he was playing a different violin by Peter Greiner, made in 1997. "I felt that the other one still lacked depth and darkness," he explained during that visit. "It had the Strad sound, which tends to be bright. This one is a Guarneri del Gesù model and has the darker, deeper Guarneri sound; it also has more power, especially on the lower strings, which was much better for the Mozart sonata we just played [K. 526]."

"The way I got this fiddle was rather interesting," he told me. "My wife and I always give a big party on New Year's Eve, and Mr. Greiner came to the last one, bringing a violin he had just made to show me. I tried it, compared it to the old Greiner, and grabbed it immediately. The next morning, I took it on a recital tour in Denmark and performed on it that night."

Somewhat dazed, I asked, "Just like that?"

He laughed. "It sounded wonderful from the first moment. You can tell what a violin sounds like just from the resonance of the open strings." The new violin does indeed sound wonderful. What did he do with the old one? "I gave it to the owner of my Strad, since it's a Strad model," he answered. "He is a violin aficionado, and he has done something really wonderful: he has ordered a whole string quartet from Peter Greiner. The instruments will probably go to a foundation and be loaned to a young quartet; now my former fiddle can be added.

"Until fairly recently," he added, "every good violinist wanted an old instrument, but because of their limited availability and correspondingly high prices, many musicians are now looking for new ones, so I think this is the first time in history that modern makers are being taken seriously and not expected merely to do repair work and build student instruments."

for "cross" and "sharp" is the same], even repeating accidental sharps within the bar. In the *Musical Offering,* there is a canon called "Rätsel-Canon" [riddle canon] written in a certain shape, partly in numbers, partly in notes; it's one page that adds up to half an hour of music. During his last years, Bach wrote only a few, very complicated pieces, like the *Musical Offering* and the *Art of the Fugue,* which are full of these intricacies. And of course we know that he liked to incorporate the notes that spell his name: B-A-C-H [the notes are B♭-A-C-B because, in German, the B is B♭ and the H is B]; he does that in the Fugue of the C-Major Solo Sonata, forward as well as backward: H-C-A-B [B-C-A-B♭].

Later composers, like Shostakovich and Berg, also spelled out their initials with notes.
And when Schumann refers to marriage (*Ehe* in German), he uses the corresponding notes (E-B-E).

What are you concentrating on now, besides Bach?
I've learned three new concertos; the one by Ligeti is, for me, the most wonderful modern violin concerto. It is tremendously touching and has a big, fabulous solo part and great orchestration. He wrote it in 1992–93; I first played it in Boston in January 1997 and again that October. Ligeti was there—it was the first time I performed a big new piece in the presence of the composer. I had a long talk with him and it was a wonderful experience. *[Tetzlaff also played the Ligeti Concerto in New York's Carnegie Hall with the London Symphony Orchestra under Pierre Boulez a few weeks before his Bach cycle, in March 2000. It was a spectacular performance.]*
    Then I played a concerto by Peter Ruzicka, a well-known German composer. That was also a good piece; I gave the first performances with a German orchestra under [Vladimir] Ashkenazy in Berlin and Frankfurt, with the composer present. The third concerto was by a Korean composer, Gyu-Bon Yi, which came out on top in a competition for a new violin concerto.

Your repertoire is adventurous, ranging from Baroque to 20th-century music. I know that several years ago you performed and recorded a Janáček Concerto.
Yes, the score was found among the composer's papers in the early 1990s. It's a fascinating, authentic work, but there are doubts about the orchestration and the organization of the material, some of which Janáček later used for his opera *The House of the Dead.*
    I also recorded the unpublished "original" version of the Beethoven Concerto. It is so difficult that the violinist who premiered it complained. Beethoven, who was not quite happy with it himself, transcribed it for piano and eventually gave it the form we know today.

Have you added any new standard literature to your repertoire lately?

Yes, the Sibelius Concerto, which I've always wanted to play. The Finnish Radio Orchestra asked me to perform it with them; we did it at the London Proms under Jukka-Pekka Salonen. Since then, I've played it again in London and Berlin.

How do you choose your repertoire?

Well, I just keep looking at our great literature and take up the pieces I love one after another. Sometimes, as with the Sibelius, the stimulus comes from outside.

I've always felt that you go very much your own way, both in your repertoire and your playing.

I think my musical education was rather different from that of most violinists. I was born in Hamburg. My family loved music—both my older siblings played instruments—so I was given the same opportunity and started on the recorder at the age of four or five. When I was six, I began to play both violin and piano, but when I was about 14, I gave up the piano, although I liked it, because I became serious about the violin and was better and faster at it.

Cylla Von Tiedemann

"I just keep looking at our great literature and take up the pieces I love one after another."

What made you get serious?

At that time, I began to study with Professor Üwe-Martin Haiberg at the Lübeck Conservatory. He was a very, very good musician, player, and teacher and became my basic musical influence, giving me a special kind of musical education. It was then that I really started to practice and work properly, but I didn't even know the violin literature: I had been interested mostly in orchestral and chamber music. When I studied a concerto, I didn't know other people's ideas about it or have their playing in my ear, so I did many things on my own, just figuring them out for myself. Maybe the results were not always completely satisfying, but they were absolutely my own. And actually, tradition is not always the final authority, and following rules is no good if they don't express the player's personality. So I learned to be myself.

Your career, too, has been rather unusual.

It started comparatively late and developed very gradually. When I was about 21, a very good agent heard one of my concerts and offered to represent me in Germany. He got me engagements, I would get reinvited, things sort of snowballed, and each year I played a little more and with better orchestras and better conductors.

Recordings

Bartók: *Violin Concerto No. 2; Violin Sonata. London Philharmonic Orchestra, Michael Gielen, cond. (Virgin Classics 59062).*

Beethoven: *Violin Concerto; Piano Concerto No. 2. Southwest German Radio Symphony Orchestra, Miochael Gielen, cond. (Point Classics/Eclipse 265062).*

Dvořák: *Violin Concerto; Lalo: Symphony espagnole. Czech Philharmonic Orchestra, Libor Pesek, cond. (VC 45022).*

Haydn: *Violin Concertos Nos. 1, 3, and 4; Violin Rondo, K. 373. Northern Sinfonia of England, Heinrich Schiff, cond. (VC 59065).*

Janáček: *Violin Concerto. Philharmonia Orchestra, L. Pesek, cond. (VC 59076).*

Mozart: *Violin Concertos; Violin Adagio K. 261; Violin Rondo K. 269; Violin Rondo K. 373. German Chamber Philharmonic Orchestra, Christian Tetzlaff, cond. (VC 2-ZDCB 45214).*

Weill: *Violin Concerto. German Chamber Philharmonic Orchestra Winds, Christian Tetzlaff, cond. (VC 45056).*

*By now, of course, the snowball is off and rolling, but you actually do
what most successful performers only say they want to do: you arrange
your concert schedule so that you don't stay away from home too long.
How do you manage?*

It's very simple. For every week I work, I must have one free; if I am
away for two weeks, I'm at home for two weeks. I end up with about
85 concerts a year, which is still quite a lot. This tour, for example, was
supposed to last four weeks, but I canceled two concerts in Florida and
got my week at home. They were kind enough to let me do that,
because their second soloist, pianist Olli Mustonen, was available to
play on those days. My only problem is that I really *want* to play all the
engagements that come along. It would have been nice to go to Florida
in November. But with a new baby at home, our third child, I'm needed there more than ever, not only to see him grow, but to help. So when
I'm home, I'm really there all day, and on the whole spend at least as
much time with my family as any normal working husband.

*Aren't you afraid of not being reengaged if you cancel or refuse engage-
ments?*

If people didn't invite me back just because I turned them down once,
I'd really be in trouble!

How much practicing do you need to learn so much new music?

When I am at home, I practice very little, usually no more than an hour
and a half a day. Neither the Guy-Bon Yi nor the Ruzicka concerto was
very difficult, and the Ligeti—well, I did practice a couple of hours a
day while I was learning that! I deliberately gave myself more than a
year to learn the Sibelius, and I still have to put more work into it. And
on tour, I am careful because I have to be ready to play in the evening.

You also play sonata recitals, don't you?

I play about seven concerts a year with pianist Matthias Kirschnereit,
and I always look forward to my annual tour with Leif-Ove Andsnes.
Playing with him is very fulfilling for me. On our last program we
played three of my favorite sonatas: Mozart's A Major, K. 526; the
Brahms No. 1, and Bartók No. 1.

*I remember your beautiful performance of the Janáček Sonata with him.
May I ask you a few questions about it? Its markings are so meticulous
yet so ambiguous—all those metronome marks. . . .*

Yes, neither the tempo- nor the metronome-markings make complete
sense. If you start counting, "Aha, this is 80, and this is twice as fast, so
it should be 160," it never comes out correctly. And sometimes you can't
even get close: for example, here it's 180 to the quarter note, and if you
play 32nd notes, that's physically impossible. It just means, "fast!" Here

it says "Tempo primo," but it's 94—that's the second tempo, not the first, so it's a bad marking. And this *meno mosso* goes from 180 to 94—that's twice as slow, not just a slight modification. I think all this was part of Janáček's very erratic but really rather nice way of composing. You feel he is constantly reacting to impulses from outside; there is never a complete classical line, there are always interruptions, which maybe he didn't anticipate himself when he started composing. His manuscripts, too, are extremely difficult to make out. I found that I had to abandon strict logical thinking with this sonata. But it's a beautiful piece; I love it.

And I love the way you play it, in concert and on your record. Tell me more about your recordings.

Well, I am no longer with Virgin Classics, because I was not satisfied with the way they promoted and distributed my records, and I could never get everything together: the right orchestras, a good hall, and enough recording time. The Mozart concerti were the last recording I made for them; I chose the orchestra but not the venue, so getting a good sound was very difficult.

In the Mozart concerti, do you play the tuttis along with the orchestra? One cannot tell on the records.

I hope not: if one could, there would be something wrong! I think I played along on some; most of the time, there was no need to with that good concertmaster. But in the *ritornellos* of the last movements, I prefer to play with the orchestra and emerge from it.

Have you recorded for any other labels?

No. Once a radio production of the original version of the Beethoven Concerto was made into a recording without my knowledge [by the Intercord label]—a catastrophe for me! It was the first time I ever recorded with an orchestra, and without a rehearsal, too! So now there is a recording of the Beethoven concerto on the market, being heavily promoted and sold quite a lot, of which I do not approve at all.

Are you planning to find another label?

Eventually, but nothing is definite at the moment.

Do you have any favorites among your repertoire?

The Romantic repertoire is my favorite—because it's so much fun to play, not because I like the music better than Mozart's or Berg's.

"Playing chamber music is really a luxury, because it takes ten times longer to prepare."

Do you have time and opportunity to play chamber music?

All my life, I've tried to play as much chamber music as possible. As you know, I spent a year at Cincinnati University, studying with Walter Levine of the La Salle Quartet, and I loved the two summers I spent at Marlboro, in Vermont. I went back to the Risö Festival in Norway again this summer; we always play a lot of beautiful music there. Of course, playing chamber music is really a luxury, because it takes ten times longer to prepare; it has to be planned ahead very carefully. The good thing is that I can do most of it at home.

Last year, I played all three piano trios by Schumann, which were always favorites of mine. I also did a chamber-music project in several places that included the Brahms Clarinet Quintet and the big, first Schoenberg String Quartet, his last so-called Romantic piece. Time takes on a completely different meaning: we had two complete weeks of rehearsals for three concerts, which is about the same amount of work I'd put into three months of concertizing. But that was the fulfillment of two dreams I'd had for a long time.

Hilary Hahn

American violinist Hilary Hahn has established herself as one of the most talented and intelligent young performers on the international concert stage. As an 11-year-old student at the Curtis Institute of Music in Philadelphia, she made her orchestral debut with the Baltimore Symphony in 1991; just four years later she received an Avery Fisher Career Grant. Her tours have included performances with the Pittsburgh Symphony, Cleveland Orchestra, New York Philharmonic, and Bavarian Radio Symphony Orchestra. Now based in Philadelphia, she pursues an active chamber-music career in addition to her solo work, performing regularly at summer festivals and with the Chamber Music Society of Lincoln Center in New York. This interview took place in April 1999, just after one such Lincoln Center concert.

Fulfilling Her Promise

Julia Zaustinsky

At 19, American violinist Hilary Hahn is one of the most impressive and musically compelling artists in the ever-growing galaxy of young virtuosos. Her virtuosity transcends technical perfection and violinistic wizardry. She is a master musician whose playing is illumined by a love for music and the need to communicate. "Music, for me, is interaction—interaction with the audience and with colleagues. I play each piece of music the way I would like to hear it if I were in the audience." On stage, her intense concentration grips the audience from the moment her bow touches the string and launches her listeners on a spellbinding musical journey. Hahn's playing speaks from the heart with an intelligence, eloquence, and nobility that places her among the great interpreters of our time.

Hahn's extraordinary musical gifts were apparent at an early age. She made her debut as soloist with the Baltimore Symphony when she was 11. Her 1993 debut with the Philadelphia Orchestra was followed by engagements with the Cleveland Orchestra, the New York Philharmonic, the Pittsburgh Symphony, and other major orchestras in the

U.S. and Europe. At 16, she completed the Curtis Institute's graduation requirements, made her Carnegie Hall debut (again with the Philadelphia Orchestra), and signed an exclusive recording contract with Sony Classical. Her first CD (Sony 62793)—a patrician performance of the last three of Bach's monumental Sonatas and Partitas for unaccompanied violin—received France's *Diapaison d'Or* for young talent. In the U.S. it became the Pick of the Month for *Stereo Review* and a bestseller on the *Billboard* classical charts.

Hahn's interest in the violin began shortly before her fourth birthday. She was taking a walk with her father in their Baltimore neighborhood when they passed a branch of the Peabody Conservatory that advertised music lessons for four-year-olds. Looking in on a lesson where a little boy was playing "Twinkle, Twinkle," Hahn was intrigued. She started taking lessons the next week. "Actually, I didn't start on the violin," she remembers. "I started on a book wrapped in wrapping paper with a ruler sticking out of it. I held that under my chin and just stood while a cassette played. I was in a Suzuki class for about a year and played the violin for the first time just after I turned four."

An engaging young woman, Hahn not only loves to perform but also enjoys talking about her early years and her life as a violinist on the international circuit. I asked Hahn how she trained for her first public performances.

After the Suzuki start, with whom did you study?

When I was five, I started to study with Klara Berkovich. She was a Russian teacher who had just immigrated from St. Petersburg, after teaching for 25 years at the Leningrad School for the Musically Gifted. I studied with her for five years at Peabody Prep. She taught me how to draw my bow, how to play double-stops, vibrato, pizzicato—basically everything you need to know to play the violin. She also taught me the basics of phrasing, so I knew what to do with a phrase and how to make something interesting. I did a lot of études with her, especially Wohlfahrt.

When I was about nine, she told me that I had done enough work to give a recital by myself. It hadn't occurred to me that I could, because I had never heard anyone do that. I went home, looked at my repertoire, and decided that she was right, I probably could. We worked toward this for about eight months. The program included a Handel Sonata, the "Siciliano" and Presto from Bach's unaccompanied Sonata in G Minor, the Wieniawski Caprice in A Minor, the Vitali Chaconne, Glière Romance, and other short pieces.

Around this time, Mrs. Berkovich told me that she had taught me as much as she felt comfortable teaching me, and it was time for me to look for another teacher. I talked with some of the teachers at the Peabody Conservatory, and one of them told me that she knew a wonderful teacher for me, Jascha Brodsky, who taught at the Curtis Institute. She suggested that I audition for Curtis. I had friends who had auditioned for Curtis and hadn't gotten in, and they were of college age. But I was entering a competition and wanted to play one of the Viotti Concertos for someone. So I went to the audition entirely for the performance experience, and I didn't expect much to come of it. But a couple of weeks later, Gary Grafman, the director of Curtis, told me that I had been accepted and that I would be studying with Jascha Brodsky. Since you can't pick your teachers at Curtis—they pick you—I was extraordinarily lucky.

Janusz Kawa

You were ten then?

Yes, and he was 83. I had a wonderful time studying with him. He told me tons of stories. He had studied with Eugène Ysaÿe in Paris in the '20s, and Ysaÿe was born in the 1850s, so there is just one generation between me and this great Belgian School. I studied with Brodsky for seven years, until he died, when he was 89 and I was 17. He took what Mrs. Berkovich had taught me and refined and developed it. He took me through the next sequence of études—Kreutzer, Sevčík, Gaviniès, Rode, and the Paganini Caprices. He taught me about 28 concertos, recital programs,

"I play each piece of music the way I would like to hear it if I were in the audience."

and lots of short pieces. He gave me a thorough technical training and, like Mrs. Berkovich, wouldn't let me go on to the next thing until what I was working on was absolutely right.

He had a kind of musical hierarchy that he wanted me to work through, with Beethoven and Brahms at the end. I wanted to do the Beethoven Concerto a couple of years too soon, according to his schedule. I would beg him to allow me to do it, promising to practice really, really hard. His response was always, "No, you must wait until you have studied all the other repertoire. Then you will be completely prepared for it." So I put a lot of time and effort into the other pieces and moved fairly quickly through the repertoire, because I wanted so badly to be able to work on Beethoven and Brahms.

Did you have to move to Philadelphia to be a Curtis student?

Curtis is very flexible, so the first two years I stayed in Baltimore. I was homeschooled at that point, in order to have time to do everything I wanted to do. During the first two years I did my homework on the road while we commuted twice a week to Philadelphia for my lessons, rehearsals, and coachings.

When I was 12, I started working toward the Curtis bachelor's degree. The dean suggested that I take college courses to fulfill my high school requirements, so I was able to kill two birds with one stone. Although I was in classes with 18-year-olds who had entered that year,

What She Plays

Hilary Hahn plays an 1864 Jean Baptiste Vuillaume violin formerly owned by the Russian violinist Samuel Lande, who was a friend and colleague of Klara Berkovich, Hahn's first teacher. Lande's heirs emigrated to the United States and, after hearing one of Hahn's early recitals, decided that she should be the instrument's next owner. Hahn's early-20th-century bows were made by the French makers Paul Jombar and Emil Miquel. She also sometimes uses a 1999 bow made by the Brazilian maker Horst John, a W.E. Hill & Sons exhibition bow, and an unidentified bow with both French and German characteristics, somewhat in the style of Vuillaume, which predates the 1940s. She uses a Pirastro Steel E string, and the three lower strings are Dominants (a regular A and G, and a Silver D).

Recordings

Barber, Samuel, and Edgar Meyer: Violin Concertos. St. Paul Chamber Orchestra, Hugh Wolff, cond. (Sony Classics CD 89029).

Beethoven: Violin Concerto; Bernstein: Serenade. Baltimore Symphony Orchestra, David Zinman, cond. (Sony Classics CD 60584).

Hilary Hahn Plays Bach: *Partitas and Sonatas for Violin (Sony Classics CD 62793).*

Janusz Kawa

I felt just like part of the family. I felt like the younger sister without the arguments. It's a great school because it's small and we all know each other. I took a lot of literature courses, Western Civ, seven years of German, and all the necessary harmony classes, music history, and counterpoint and keyboard harmony, and completed the Curtis requirements for graduation when I was 16.

Janusz Kawa

But I didn't graduate. I loved the school so much I couldn't bring myself to leave. Once you leave you can't come back, so I decided to stay as long as I could. There were a lot of classes that interested me that I hadn't taken yet—I took a poetry writing class, a fiction writing class, several English classes, and continued with German. [Hahn graduated from Curtis in May 1999.]

Have you continued to study the violin with a teacher?

After Mr. Brodsky died, Jaime Laredo became my teacher and one of my mentors for a while. The years between 17 and 19 or 20 are transitional— I didn't feel like studying full-time with anyone, but I also didn't feel ready to be out on my own yet. When Mr. Laredo was in town, I would play for him. I didn't see him that much, but it was nice to know that he was there and that I could go to him for advice when I needed to.

"I've learned a lot from working with other musicians."

Who are some of the other musicians who have been important in your artistic development?

David Zinman, the conductor of the Baltimore Symphony, has been my mentor since I was ten. The Baltimore Symphony was very important in my early development. People there advised me not to do too many things too soon, not to be an overly busy prodigy type, not to go to management too soon, not to record before I was ready, and to stay in school. All of this was very good advice.

Also, Lorin Maazel was an important mentor. When I was about 15, I played with him on tour with the Bavarian Radio Symphony Orchestra in Europe, principally in Germany but also in Holland, England, and Scotland. I worked with him on a regular basis.

I've learned a lot from working with other musicians. I had a great experience in January [1999] when I got to play the Mozart Sinfonia Concertante with Yuri Bashmet and Josef Suk conducting the Josef Suk Chamber Orchestra. This was like a dream come true; the two are great musicians. I also get to work with a lot of wonderful people at Marlboro, as well as at CMS Two [Lincoln Center Chamber Music Society's "junior" program]. And playing this week for the first time

with Joseph Silverstein as a violinist [see profile on page 25] has been
really fun. When I was 13, I played a New Year's concert in Utah with
him conducting. It was my first concert west of the Mississippi.

*Who are the historic violinists whose playing has had an influence on
your playing?*
When I was really young, I listened a lot to Jascha Heifetz and Arthur
Grumiaux. Later on, I became interested in Mischa Elman, Fritz
Kreisler, and Nathan Milstein. I listen to a lot of old recordings. I like
the fact that they're straight performances and haven't been spliced
together. In my own recordings I've tried to record large segments, so as
to have a whole interpretation.

How did you select the repertoire for your first CDs?
Bach was the composer that immediately came to mind, not only
because it's such great music, but because I've played Bach more than
any other composer. My father sang in a chorus and I grew up listening
to tapes of Bach's choral music. I started playing the Sonatas and Partitas
when I was eight and have played some solo Bach every day since then.

This proved to be a good choice for a first CD because there was
time to get everything the way I wanted it. Sometimes we would start
recording at six or seven at night and go until five in the morning. We
had the freedom to work as late as we wanted every night because there
were no union rules or anyone else's schedule to work around.

For my first orchestral CD, I really wanted to play the Beethoven
Concerto because I've played it more than any other concerto and I feel
most comfortable with it. But this is one of the greatest concertos ever
written, and I had to think what to pair with it. As I was taking the train
to New York one day, I looked at my list of repertoire. I skimmed past
Bernstein a couple of times and then just on a whim thought, what
about Beethoven and Bernstein? I almost said it out loud. Instantly it
made sense to me. They were both 36 when they wrote their concertos.
They were both pianists and conductors, as well as composers. Both
pieces are very large-scale, though they are almost complete opposites
in form. The Beethoven has standard movements with classic cadenza
placement. The Bernstein Serenade is in five movements, two of which
are divided, and the cadenza is in the fourth movement. It is based on
Plato's *Symposium,* with movements named after the great philosophers.
It's a piece of shifting moods—it can be jazzy, or jaunty, or cheeky, but
also beautifully lyrical. It's a perfect complement to the Beethoven.

*Do you have a special repertoire you play in certain kinds of settings?
For instance, I know you do a lot of outreach to grade-school students.*
Yes. It's hard to count on there being a good piano available in a school,
and I don't always have colleagues, so I generally play works for unaccompanied violin. I always play Bach, a slow and a fast movement.

When I first started doing this, I thought that there was no way that they were going to sit still. But the music casts a spell. They really like it. There's also an Ernst transcription of the *Erlkönig* for solo violin that I enjoy playing for kids. I tell them about the great German poet Goethe, whose work was set to music by a great German composer, Schubert. They find it interesting to listen to the different voices and how they interact in the solo violin version. I also show them harmonics and violinistic tricks that they may never have seen before. There is a Sevčík left-hand pizzicato exercise that I used to do every night that they find very intriguing.

I want to give students an idea of what can be done with the violin. But I also want to give them enough time to make up their own questions and ask them at their own pace. I love meeting the kids because they are really open to what they are hearing. They are curious to know what my life is like, whether I get lonely, whether I like traveling. I think many of them have never heard of anyone playing the violin as a career.

How did you become involved in these musical encounters?

When I was 11, I won a Concerto Soloists of Philadelphia competition. Part of the project involved going to play in the inner-city schools in Philadelphia. Two years ago, I joined the Lincoln Center Chamber Music Society Two program. They do a lot of outreach work with schools all over New York and I visited a number of schools with them. There were some really good educators in charge and I learned a lot from them about how to interact with children. Last year I did a program with a third-grade class in upstate New York. I knew the teacher and was staying in her home while I was getting ready for a local recital. She asked me to visit her class, and I really enjoyed it. They were doing a geography project in which they asked everyone they knew who was traveling anywhere to send postcards from the cities they visited, to learn about these places and have some connection with cities around the world. I asked if they would like me to send postcards from every place I went that year, and their response was "Yeah!" So I did, and they wrote me back letters.

What were some of the cities from which you wrote?

Warsaw, Zurich, Jerusalem, and many others. I loved being in Jerusalem. It's very interesting to watch cultures that are parallel but don't mix. There are four quarters—Christian, Muslim, Jewish, and Armenian. As you walk through the old city, which is actually quite small, you see orthodox Jews walking to the Wailing Wall. The next moment you're in the middle of an Arab market with Arab music in the street and spices on the side of the road. It's a really, really fascinating place.

Was this the genesis of "Hilary's Journal" on the Web?

Yes. At the end of the year, the teacher compiled some 30 postcards into a book, and I read through it and decided that I wanted to do this again. The problem was that the teacher was retiring. Then I wondered if this could be carried out on a larger scale, so I talked with Sony and we set up something on my Web site [www.hilaryhahn.com] with three schools, two in New York City and one in Los Angeles. Students send me questions and I write the answers and put them on my Web site. It has my schedule, biography, and "Hilary's Journal," which consists of these electronic "postcards" from around the world. Every week or so I try to send a postcard to my Web site. There are some pictures that I take with a digital camera that Sony loaned me, and I send them in by e-mail. The Sony people set them up on my site.

When I was in L.A., I met the students at the Colbert School, one of the three schools I work with. In New York, I visited the students at P.S. 183. We started the session with a little girl playing a piece for me and the class. I really like listening to the kids.

Do you have some advice for kids like these, who are studying the violin?
Yes: practice slowly. It is hard to learn to do this, but it is really important, especially for accurate intonation.

Do you have your own daily routine of scales or technical exercises?
I've always done Bach and some kind of technical exercise every day. And right now I'm working on the Ernst Polyphonic Etudes. He wrote six—the "Last Rose" is the last one. I had never heard of the other five. I think that they're good pieces and I'm working on them as technical studies.

What about scales and arpeggios?
I still do scales and arpeggios on a fairly regular basis, but I mainly try to work on technique in context. Every piece has scales and arpeggios. I play the scale passages slowly, making sure that I have good fingerings and know what I'm doing.

How do you prepare your season?
Usually I schedule eight different concertos in a year, as well as chamber music and a recital with as many new pieces in it as possible. Recitals are generally booked in one long tour. Last season I was on the road playing recitals for five and a half weeks. I played in Italy and Lithuania for the first time, at Wigmore Hall in London, several places in Germany, and throughout the U.S. I try to schedule three new concertos each year, and I try to prepare new material about a year in advance.

What are some of your projects for the coming season?
I'm very excited about the concerts that I'll be doing with Hugh Wolff and the St. Paul Chamber Orchestra. We'll be premiering the Edgar Meyer Violin Concerto that I commissioned. I've never done a com-

mission before. I was in the orchestra for the Ned Rorem Concerto for the Left Hand, so I've seen how a commission is put together in its final stages. But I've never worked from the beginning, getting a few pages at a time, trying to imagine what is going on in the orchestra, and actually finding out how it's all put together. It has been a very interesting process for me, and an eye-opener. Now I approach the other concertos I'm working on from a different perspective. I hope to commission more new works for violin and orchestra.

What do you enjoy doing when you're not playing the violin?

Oh, lots of things. I like movies. I went to see the Marcel Marceau show here in New York and I went to hear Garrick Ohlsson's recital that took place just before mine. I love reading and writing. I enjoy exploring new cities and meeting new people. I take ballet classes whenever I can, I go to the gym, I like to swim and ride my bike. And last summer [1998] I did something that was a big departure: I went to Middlebury College, Vermont, for their intensive language program in German. I think I practiced the violin about an hour a day, if that. It was really fun—I had a regular college experience for a little while.

As a young American artist building an international career, how do you view the future of classical music in America?

I think it has a big future. We have a lot of great musicians and there is so much great music. It's a matter of bringing music to people who ordinarily wouldn't come to concerts.

Once I visited an inner-city school in Chicago where University of Chicago graduate students talked to kids about music on a regular basis, particularly opera. The kids had memorized the entire plot of Verdi's Aida. They knew every character, what every character did, and how the opera was put together. One little boy raised his hand and asked me, "Did Verdi write anything for the violin?" It made me aware of the impact professional musicians and music students can have on education, and the importance of getting involved.

Vadim Repin

Siberian violinist Vadim Repin won his first competition at five and a half, the Wieniawski International Competition at 11, and the Queen Elisabeth Competition at 17. Since then, he has sustained his highly successful career through the extraordinary quality of his playing, which combines stunning virtuosity with poetic sensibility, youthful vitality, and emotional involvement. He has performed with leading conductors and orchestras, including the Chicago Symphony, Cleveland Orchestra, Los Angeles Philharmonic, Orchestre de Paris, and the Royal Concertgebouw Orchestra. As is clear in this late 1999 interview, he is also a devoted chamber musician.

Citizen of the World

Edith Eisler

In the popular imagination, Siberia has always evoked visions of a vast, desolate area of ice, snow, and prison camps. No more. In recent years Siberia, like Ukraine several decades earlier, has become a hotbed of astounding musical talents, especially violin prodigies. However, while the Ukrainian wunderkindern (such as Nathan Milstein and pianist Vladimir Horowitz) got most of their training in Moscow or St. Petersburg, the Siberian ones get it right at home in Novosibirsk. The sudden appearance of a succession of extraordinary players (including Maxim Vengerov and Anton Barachovsky) points to the presence of an extraordinary teacher, and indeed the arrival of Zakhar Bron at the Novosibirsk Conservatory has been a major factor in the discovery of Siberia's treasure trove of violin talents. As his students' careers have blossomed, so has his reputation; they have made one another famous. One of the most gifted, appealing, and arresting performers to emerge from Bron's tutelage is Vadim Repin. Born in Novosibirsk in 1971, he began to take lessons with Bron at the age of seven and continued for 13 years. When Bron was offered a guest professorship in Lübeck, Germany, on condition that he bring along some of his students, Repin went with him.

Though Repin started winning major competitions when he was only 11, his international reputation was established when he won the prestigious Queen Elisabeth Competition in Brussels at the age of 17. His career has flourished ever since, taking him all over the world to perform recitals, chamber music, and concertos with leading orchestras and conductors. His repertoire ranges from classical to contemporary and he has a large, award-winning discography to his credit.

Repin has visited New York many times as soloist with various American and European orchestras. From the first time I heard him, it was clear that he was an extraordinary player, and that impression has been confirmed and reinforced by each subsequent appearance as well as by his recordings. His tone is radiantly beautiful, warm, variable, and powerful, and unbroken by instrumental limitations such as changes of bow, string, or position. He has a spectacular technique, remarkable in its apparently limitless facility and infallible security, and a virtuoso's natural flair without a virtuoso's mannerisms or exaggerations. He tosses off the most incredible acrobatics with an effortless ease that must be heard and seen to be believed, and he seems to have fun besides.

However, what is most captivating about his playing is his innate musicality, his unerring sense of style, his irresistible charm, and his ability to make even pure bravura pieces sound like music. His formidable technical resources are entirely at the service of the composer, and he combines respect for the score with a strongly felt personal response to the music, from inward expressiveness to fiery, passionate abandon.

I had a chance to talk with him on one of his rare free days shortly after this concert. Unspoiled by his rapid early success, he is natural and unassuming and radiates as much charm in person as in his playing. In contrast to his severely dignified stage presence, his manner in private is relaxed and easy, full of humor and an almost palpable warmth. He talks about his chamber-music partners and other musicians with admiration and affection, and he discusses music with passionate seriousness, but when he speaks of himself and his thriving career, it is with a self-deprecating laugh and a twinkle in his eye. Widely traveled, he is a true cosmopolitan and versed in several languages, having lived in Germany and then in Amsterdam after finishing his studies. For the last two years, he has made his home in Monaco on the French Riviera.

How did you get started on the violin?

I first started to be interested in musical toys when I was three. I always wanted a xylophone—anything with which to make music—and I found some melodies on it, songs I knew or lullabies my mother had sung to me. When I was four, my father gave me my first real instrument, a small accordion. My mother decided I must have some talent and took me to the music school in my hometown when I was five. Not being a musician, she had no idea what I should study, but she thought I should continue with the accordion because I could already play it.

But the class was full and, since I was so young, we were advised to try the violin. After six months, I won a competition for young children and played on stage for the first time.

That's when most students are still learning where to put their fingers. What did you play?

I don't know, some Vivaldi and some small pieces—it was just for children. The next year I won it again, and then, when I was seven, I started taking lessons with Professor Bron. He was my real teacher.

Is he the reason that so many fabulous fiddle players are suddenly coming out of Siberia?

[*Laughs.*] Yes, one of the big reasons, I think.

Why and when did he go to Novosibirsk, of all places?

He came about three or four years before I met him. He was very young, in his early 30s. He had an advanced degree from Moscow Conservatory, where people take their studies very seriously and perhaps get a better education than elsewhere. But I think it really makes little difference whether you go to a more or less prestigious school; how much you learn depends mostly on your own will. So I guess Bron came to Novosibirsk because he wanted to get far away from Moscow—which is sort of the center of musical life in Russia—and start something of his own, something new.

Yehudi Menuhin was Repin's mentor for several major concertos.

Did he establish his own school?

No, he taught in the conservatory, but he had his own class and worked in his own way.

Does he use his own material?

He used scales and études, Kreutzer, of course, and Dont. [*Chuckles.*] I think my first étude was Paganini's No. 16, but he didn't want me to know that it was Paganini and he only gave me the first part, so he wrote it down as an exercise. I was about eight years old then.

Does he have a specific method?

His method. . . . I think the most important part of it was his ability to explain as well as to show things. His way of teaching is very clear and precise, very pointed, very quick.

Another important thing was that he gave his students opportunities to perform. He was forever organizing concerts for his class. That was very nice, because the most difficult part of teaching children is to get them to practice, not just to play and have fun. And you can't perform

What He Plays

For the last three years, Vadim Repin has played on an Antonio Stradivari violin made in Cremona in 1708, given to him on an indefinite loan by the Stradivari Society in Chicago.

"It's called the 'Ruby' for its reddish varnish, and it's a magnificent violin," Repin says, "one of the most beautiful Strads I've seen. I love it."

He knows its owner, whom he calls the patrón. "But," he explains, "though some of the patróns want to be known, this one wants to remain incognito. I think it's a beautiful idea to lend out these violins; I am very happy to play on mine and I hope they are also happy to let me use it."

"I have three bows: one by Kittel, a Russian maker whose bows Heifetz used to play all his life, a Maline, a student of Peccatte, and a Pfretzschner that I use for practicing. My G and D strings are Dominant; the E is Westminster, the thickest kind. I don't remember what the A is."

Before he got the "Ruby," Repin played a Stradivari given to him by a Swiss patrón named Olivier Jacques. "The violin was called the 'Smith' and was also very beautiful," Repin says. "Before that, I had a Strad from the Russian State Collection, the 'ex-Wieniawski.' On my most recent recording, where I play the Lalo Symphonie espagnole, Sarasate premiered it on the same violin, the 'Ruby' Strad."

Recordings

Lalo: Symphonie Espagnol; Ravel: Tzigane; Chausson: Poème. London Symphony Orchestra, Kent Nagano, cond. (Erato 27314).

Medtner: Sonata No. 3; Ravel: Sonata. (Erato 15110).

Mozart: Concertos Nos. 2, 3, and 5. Vienna Chamber Orchestra, Yehudi Menuhin, cond. (Erato 21660).

Prokofiev: Sonatas Nos. 1 and 2; Five Melodies. With Boris Berezovsky, piano (Erato 10698).

Shostakovich: Concerto No. 1; Prokofiev: Concerto No. 2. Hallé Orchestra, Kent Nagano, cond. (Erato 10696).

Tchaikovsky: Concerto in D Major; Sibelius: Concerto in D Minor. London Symphony Orchestra, Emmanuel Krivine, cond. (Erato 98537).

Tchaikovsky: Piano Trio in A Minor; Shostakovich: Piano Trio No. 2 in E Minor. With Dmitry Yablonsky, cello; Boris Berezovsky, piano (Erato 17875).

Tutta Bravura: Music of Bazzini, Paganini, Sarasate, and others (Erato 25487).

Vadim Repin au Louvre: Works by Debussy, Lalo, Ravel, and others (Erato 26411).

if you aren't prepared and haven't learned your piece, so to play in a concert is a goal, an achievement. To study with him you had to work very hard; he was constantly pushing you.

When I was about 11, I started taking real competitions. This was very important, because it was the only way of being noticed in Russia at that time, especially if you came from Siberia. So we went to Poland for the Wieniawski Competition, for young musicians up to age 19, I think. They gave me all the prizes they had. I remember I was extremely happy because I got all the money of the competition. [*Laughs heartily.*] I went shopping for the first time in my life, and I felt rich!

Thierry Cohen

And rewarded for all the hard work, too. How much did you practice?

Well, by the time I was 14, things got more serious. Professor Bron kept pushing me to learn more difficult things, and he was right; it made a good balance. So I practiced about five hours a day. I would learn something like Paganini's "La Campanella" in five days and perform it on the sixth.

Did you go to school?

Yes, at first I went to normal school—I mean music school where they taught everything. But once I started traveling a lot I also had private teachers to help me study some subjects, for example mathematics and literature, in more detail and more quickly and seriously.

The Queen Elisabeth Competition prize boosted Repin's already international career.

I've often wondered whether the famous Russian school of violin playing, which was more or less started by Leopold Auer, is still being taught.

I don't know about a Russian school; I would rather say there is a strong Russian tradition. And the teaching tradition is a very important part of it. I know it's being carried on by a lot of people who love teaching and are concentrating on it. There have always been great, great Russian violinists—Jascha Heifetz, David Oistrakh—but of course there are incredible musicians, and not-so-incredible musicians, everywhere, not only in Russia. But above all, music and violin playing are taken much more seriously in Russia than in Europe or America; people have a different attitude. In the old Soviet Union, music was a very prestigious profession and also one of the most lucrative.

So you took the Queen Elisabeth Competition, diving into the biggest of them all.

If not the biggest, certainly the hardest and longest, in terms of repertoire and duration. [*Grins.*] Yes, that was a big one, a painful one. It lasts

30 days, and you play three rounds. After the second round, they take you to a special house where you have six days to study a contemporary piece written especially for the contest. There is no way in the world you can guess anything about it, what it will be or could be like.

Thierry Cohen

"The most important thing in chamber music is to feel each other."

The one I played was a concerto by a Belgian composer; I don't remember his name. I was so happy to forget that piece. [*Laughs.*] I had nightmares about it for a long time afterward.

What did winning this competition do for you and your career?

I think it gave me a start and helped me to be noticed and invited to play in many places in Europe much sooner than would have been possible without it. It also helped me to gain self-discipline.

You seem to have had plenty of self-discipline already.

Yes, but this was different. . . . It was the first time I had traveled and lived without my parents, so that was a big change for me. The next year, when I moved to Germany, my parents came with me. But Brussels is still one of the most special cities on this planet for me. Just spending almost two months there made me feel so alive! I have great memories of it and try to go back to Belgium as often as possible.

As for my career—I think the prize gave it a certain push, but I've never paid any attention to developing my career, so I don't really know what that means. I know what it means to play your instrument, to improve yourself, to improve the quality, the caliber of your partners, the people you work with, but the career itself is the result of many things, many people coming together. So I leave thinking about that to somebody else, to my managers perhaps; they know better than I what the prize did for my career.

Did you get management through the prize or did you have one before?

I already had one; we just continued as before, only faster and flying higher, so to speak. I had played in Europe many times before, on the Bavarian Radio in Munich, in West Berlin, which still existed at that time. I had even played in Carnegie Hall in New York in 1988.

But, you know, I did get one big thing out of winning the Brussels competition. I stayed in Germany for so many years because it was the only country that allowed me to live there permanently. With a Russian passport, it was very difficult to get residency anywhere in Europe, especially Western Europe. Having studied in Germany, I knew some people there and that made it easier. But after a few years, it became impossible to carry on the professional life I lead on a Russian document, because it turned out that every time I played a concert in another country, I needed a visa, and to get one I had to visit the consulate every time to apply for it. Since not every city has a consulate, I sometimes had to fly a long way just to get permission to enter the country. It was complete chaos. I had two engagement books: one for my concerts, the other for appointments at embassies and consulates. So I finally decided to appeal to the Belgian queen, Fabiola, and she was kind enough to give me Belgian citizenship. Since Belgium is part of the European Community, I have a European passport and can go anywhere without a visa and without a problem.

You mean you are now a citizen of the world.

Yes! Of course, having won the Brussels prize made it easier to approach the queen, but it was [the late violinist] Yehudi Menuhin who helped me to write the letter and explain the situation.

How did you meet Menuhin?

Aha! I met Menuhin because we had the same manager. At that time, I was no longer studying with Bron, and I had recently learned the Brahms Concerto and was supposed to play it in London and Germany. I was very nervous about it, so I asked the manager if Maestro Menuhin might listen to me for maybe 15 minutes and give me some advice before I performed it for the first time. He did, and then he was also the first one to whom I played the Beethoven Concerto, so he became a sort of mentor to me in the greatest concertos. And later we met again and started spending time and also playing together a lot.

And then, in Vienna, we recorded three Mozart concertos with Menuhin conducting the Vienna Chamber Orchestra, an incredible orchestra. That was a big thing for me, also emotionally; I was very happy to work with him and had a great time. We just received a German award for that recording [the Echo Klassik Award of 1999, with Repin named Instrumentalist of the Year].

What other memorable collaborations have you had?

Well, about half a year ago, I did a German tour with [Mstislav] Rostropovich conducting, and that was incredible. We played Shostakovich's Violin Concerto No. 1—

—which you have recorded, haven't you?

Yes, with the Hallé Orchestra under Kent Nagano, but that was a few years ago and I play it quite differently now. Just from the way Rostropovich was conducting, I knew there were a lot of things in my playing that I wanted to improve. That was another big step forward for me, musically.

And by the way, since then I've been playing the Finale in the original version. In every edition, the orchestra plays the main theme for about 24 bars, but Rostropovich brought me the manuscript, and there the violin plays the main theme. Shostakovich changed it because Oistrakh, for whom it was written, begged him to give the soloist a bit of a rest after that huge cadenza—just 10 or 15 seconds, so he could relax and feel the blood flowing in his right hand again. But we decided to try to change it back, whatever the cost, and with training it is possible. In this concerto, you never get a rest, not from the first note; its tension and intensity are incredible.

That certainly came through in the performance I heard. Tell me about your chamber-music collaborations. Who are your partners?

It varies. I really don't want to establish my own chamber group, so I do most of my chamber-music playing at festivals, usually in the summer. There are dozens of festivals to choose from and they are all happy to have you come. Some are so special that I keep going back to them. One meets so many great artists there: [cellist] Mischa Maisky, [violist] Yuri Bashmet; last summer in Verbier we had, among others, [conductor and pianist] Jimmy Levine and [cellist] Lynn Harrell.

When do you rehearse?

We plan the programs beforehand and practice our parts, and when we get there we have three days to rehearse—

—and fight.

[*Laughs.*] More or less, yes. And there's time to enjoy the concerts, our own and those of the others. It's beautiful; I love playing chamber music, especially with such partners.

I have a wonderful record of yours, Vadim Repin au Louvre. Was that the result of one of those festivals?

Yes, it was recorded live during a concert series called Vadim Repin and His Friends at the Louvre in Paris, which has a beautiful new auditorium with very nice acoustics, perfect for chamber music. It seats about 600 or 700 people and has a big season. They gave me carte blanche to do whatever I wanted in five concerts during 11 days, so I invited my closest friends to play, have a good time in Paris, and celebrate the New Year together. And once we started rehearsing, we had an idea: Why don't we just record everything? So we put up a microphone and at the end we chose a few pieces, usually one from each concert, to put on the record. The concerts were completely sold out; 200 or 300 people had to be turned away.

Do you have a regular pianist for your recitals?

I have two with whom I play a lot: Alexander Melnikov and Boris Berezovsky. Melnikov is a very good pianist and a fine artist with a very literate, serious attitude toward music. That's very special and I respect it very much, because I also think one should start learning a piece by a close examination of the score, of what the composer wrote and what he meant. Of course you have your interpretation, and you can let the music go through your feelings, your emotions, your soul, or whatever you want to call it, but the basis, the foundation of it all is the score. A lot of times you hear people play as if they were reproducing what they've heard just by ear, or from memory, without paying attention to what's in the music. It may be passionate or beautiful, but it's not right; in the end it can make the music awkward or unbalanced.

And Berezovsky, too, is an extremely good pianist. We travel and work together a lot, and I've also recorded with him. We have a trio with [cellist] Dmitry Yablonsky; we made a recording of the Tchaikovsky and Shostakovich Trios, which also came out of a concert at the Louvre, and we are planning a concert at La Scala in Milan, a very nice place to play. We did a tour of Japan recently, combined with my orchestra and recital tour. We hadn't played together for a while, and every time you meet again, each of you has changed and developed. But the basics remain the same. We know the program, and the most important thing in chamber music is to feel each other; then you can just make music together.

Do you make cuts in the Finale of the Tchaikovsky Trio?

[*Hesitates.*] Yes. Sometimes it might seem that, with the cuts, it loses its purpose as the final step, the summation of the piece. But then, if you play the whole movement, it just gets too long; there is no development, it merely repeats itself. And the Coda becomes more weighty with the cuts. I've tried playing it both ways, and I still prefer the cuts.

How many concerts a year do you play?

I don't know, close to 100—it's a lot. It's very difficult to create a balance over time. You have to plan two or three years ahead, to have a perspective of what you are doing, but sometimes the more interesting offers come along later, because the budgets of some orchestras, as well as some festivals, are not settled until the last moment. By then you are already booked up, but you don't want to turn down these invitations, because you like them and the projects are exciting. But you cannot cancel the engagements you've already accepted; that wouldn't be polite. So you add more concerts and it gets to be too much.

Do you ever get tired of traveling?

[*Pause.*] Yes, I do. Of course one gets tired. But it's part of my life and I accept it, even if I'm not particularly happy when I'm very tired. So I take holidays and try to rest and restore myself, like these two days I'm taking off to spend in New York.

Everything you do has its good and its negative side. I made my choice and I don't regret it.

Kyung-Wha
Chung

Kyung-Wha Chung began her international career in 1967, and now, more than 30 years later, the intensity of her playing is as impressive as it's ever been. Born into a musical family in Korea, she started playing the violin at age six and studied with a formidable array of teachers, including Ivan Galamian and Joseph Szigeti. She has performed around with world with such distinguished conductors as André Previn, Sir Georg Solti, Riccardo Muti, Bernard Haitink, Lorin Maazel, Daniel Barenboim, and Claudio Abbado. The recipient of several Gramophone awards, she has also been given South Korea's highest honor, the medal of Civil Merit. In addition to performing as a soloist, she plays regularly with her brother, conductor and pianist Myung-Whun Chung, and her sister, cellist Myung-Wha Chung, in the Chung Trio, which has been honored by the United Nations.

Known for her natural reticence, Chung nevertheless displays her great passion and intelligence when discussing music. In this interview, held in early 1997 in Nottingham, England, during a concert tour, she shares her complex feelings about performing and recording.

Live Wire

Andrew Palmer

More than a quarter of a century after she became world famous, Kyung-Wha Chung still fascinates. It's not just her fastidiousness, her seriousness, and her elusiveness, but the knowledge that beneath the ice-cool exterior there is white-hot musical passion.

That's why, to fully appreciate her artistry, you have to watch her perform, not just listen to her. There's no display of histrionics for its own sake, but the excitement on her face and the energy in her body are visible evidence that she lives the music she's playing.

She's much the same in conversation because she tends to find words inadequate when talking about music, which is rooted so deeply in her that she'd probably prefer to answer questions by playing the violin rather than talking. Like many artists of the first rank, she can appear alternately shy and aloof, but she can also suddenly become extremely animated, especially when discussing a favorite work or interpretation. At such moments she beams with pleasure, and all her reserve, if not her enigmatic quality, disappears.

Part of her intrigue derives from the fact that until recently she appeared less prominent as an artist. After the excitement of her first decade, things seemed to go rather quiet, but now there are signs that she's regaining something of the high profile she enjoyed in the 1970s and early '80s. Has she really been away? And if so, where and why?

The city of Nottingham in the English Midlands seems an unlikely place to find her, particularly on a bleak February afternoon. She's here on tour with the English Chamber Orchestra and is traveling alone, having left her family home in Atlantic City [she is now based in New York City]. But England, where she had a renowned debut, has many happy memories for her and she's enjoying renewed contact with her public here. "They are very faithful," she explains. "After the concert yesterday, some ladies were waiting at the artists' door, and one of them showed me a ticket I'd signed. She said, 'You know, this was 22 years ago!' I replied, 'You mean *two* years ago?' 'No, 22!' I told her, 'Please don't wait so long before you come to see me again!'"

Because Chung looks much younger than her years—she was born in 1947—it's hard to believe that 1997 saw the 40th anniversary of her concerto debut in Seoul. Of course, she was only nine years old at that concert in 1957, and even more astonishing is the fact that she'd been playing the violin for only about two years at the time. At 13 she left Korea to study at the Juilliard School, and she went on to win the Leventritt Competition in New York, sharing the award with Pinchas Zukerman.

When she burst onto the international music scene shortly afterward in 1970, part of her initial appeal was arguably the novelty of being the first young female Asian violinist to achieve superstardom. Today, of course, Sarah Chang and Midori, among others, are enjoying similar success even younger, and the phenomenon causes Chung some concern. "Everyone needs time to reflect and to be protected from public life, and yet it all happens at an incredible pace. I've gone through it, so I know what it's like. And now they start very, very early. I know that players like [Yehudi] Menuhin and Ruggiero Ricci started early, but the pace was totally different then. They still had time to dream, to be on their own, to develop."

Chung was 22 when she first came to the U.K. and played the Tchaikovsky Concerto with the London Symphony Orchestra under its new principal conductor, André Previn. It was an extraordinary debut, not least because it hadn't been planned. Itzhak Perlman was booked to play but had to cancel when his wife went into labor, so Chung stepped in. Unaware of how difficult it can be for a young musician to make a London debut, she simply flew in and gave one. It was a turning point in her career.

"When I showed up at the rehearsal André was almost upset," she remembers, "because I was replacing Itzhak Perlman without his knowledge. There was also a mix-up over rehearsal times, so only about 40 members of the orchestra were there. André said, 'This is unfair for this young artist. Why don't we arrange another date and change the program?' I suggested that since the orchestra knew the Tchaikovsky Concerto, and as I thought I was prepared, why not just do it?

"The excitement that evening was unbelievable. Everyone was sitting on the edge of their seats because we'd hardly had a rehearsal. It was a benefit concert, and critics don't normally write about those, but there was this review the next day, and immediately the LSO's tour spread all over the country."

Chung worked with Riccardo Muti and Norman Carol of the Philadelphia Orchestra on a 1988 recording of the Dvořák Violin Concerto.

News of the extraordinary young violinist soon reached Decca Records. An audition was arranged in London's Kingsway Hall, whose old upright piano was so flat that Chung had to retune all her strings. The tapes went to Ray Minshull, then head of the company's classical division. He was stunned by what he heard. "What struck me right away was that the balance of her playing—all the passion and emotion—is in the lower strings. That's important for a violinist, but rare. With the possible exception of Joshua Bell, no one else has that incredible intensity low down. She's still the most exciting violinist I've ever heard."

Chung recorded the Tchaikovsky and Sibelius concertos for Decca, but this first recording was no more a part of Chung's career plan than a U.K. debut, for at the time competition winners didn't automatically go into the studio as they do today. In fact, she found the idea of committing *anything* to disc almost unthinkable. Performing in public was her obsession—as it remains today—and recording was something to be scheduled way in the future after her repertoire had been thoroughly "played in." Only recently has she

Recordings

Bach: Partita No. 2; Sonata No. 3 (Decca CD 440031-2).

Bach: A Musical Offering, Sonata for Flute and Violin, Trio Sonata for Two Flutes, BWV 1039. With James Galway, flute; P. Moll, harpsichord (RCA Red Seal "Papillon Collection" 6517-2-RG).

Bartók: Concerto Nos. 1 and 2. Chicago Symphony Orchestra, Sir Georg Solti, cond. (London 425015-2).

Bartók: Violin Concerto No. 2; Rhapsodies Nos. 1 and 2. City of Birmingham Symphony Orchestra, Sir Simon Rattle, cond. (EMI Classics CDC 754211-2).

Beethoven: Violin Concerto, Op. 61; Bruch: Violin Concerto in G Minor. Royal Concertgebouw/London Philharmonic Orchestras, Tennstedt, cond. (EMI Classics CDC 754072-2).

Beethoven: Violin Concerto, Op. 61; Bruch: Scottish Fantasy. Vienna Philharmonic Orchestra, Kirill Kondrashin, cond.; Royal Philharmonic Orchestra, Rudolf Kempe, cond. (London "Jubilee" 425035-2).

Beethoven: Violin Concerto, Op. 61; Mendelssohn: Violin Concerto, Op. 64; Tchaikovsky: Violin Concerto. Vienna Philharmonic, Kirill Kondrashin, cond.; Montreal Symphony Orchestra, Charles Dutoit, cond. (London "Ovation" CD 430752-2).

Beethoven: Violin Concerto. Royal Concertgebouw Orchestra, Klaus Tennstedt, cond. (EMI 991231-3, VHS video; 991231-1, laser disc).

Beethoven: Piano Trios Nos. 6 and 7. With Myung-Whun Chung, piano; Mung-Wha Chung, cello (EMI Classics CDC 55187).

Brahms: Violin Sonatas, Opp. 78, 100, and 108. With Peter Frankl, piano (EMI Classics CDC 5 562032).

Bruch: Violin Concerto in G Minor, Scottish Fantasia. Royal Philharmonic, Rudolf Kempe, cond. (Decca CD 448597-2).

Dvořák: Violin Concerto; Romance. Philadelphia Orchestra, Riccardo Muti, cond. (EMI Classics CDC 749858-2).

Dvořák: Violin Concerto. Philadelphia Orchestra, Riccardo Muti, cond. (EMI Classics CDC 69806).

Elgar: Violin Concerto; Salut d'Amour; La Capricieuse. London Philharmonic, Sir Georg Solti, cond. (Decca CD 421388-2).

Franck: Sonata. With Radu Lupu, piano (London 421154-2).

*Prokofiev: Violin Concertos Nos. 1 and 2; Stravinsky: Violin Concerto.
London Symphony Orchestra, André Previn, cond. (London "Jubilee"
425003-2).*

*Respighi: Sonata; Strauss: Violin Sonata. With Krystian Zimmerman,
piano (Deutsche Grammophon 427617-2).*

*Saint-Saëns: Violin Concertos Nos. 1 and 3; Vieuxtemps: Violin Concerto
No. 5; Chausson: Poème (Decca CD 448128-2).*

*Saint-Saëns: Havanaise, Introduction and Rondo Capriccioso, Op. 28;
Tchaikovsky: Violin Concerto. Royal Philharmonic Orchestra, Charles
Dutoit, cond. (London "Jubilee" 425021-2).*

*Souvenirs. Dvorak, Bach, Kreisler, and other. With Hamar Golan, piano
(EMI Classics CDC 5 568272).*

*Tchaikovsky: Violin Concerto; Sibelius: Violin Concerto. London
Symphony Orchestra, André Previn, cond. (London "The Classic Sound"
425080-2).*

*Tchaikovsky: Violin Concerto. Montreal Symphony Orchestra, Charles
Dutoit, cond. (London 41001-2).*

What She Plays

*Kyung-Wha Chung plays a Guarneri del Gesù violin made in 1735. Her
bow was made by the 19th-century Mirecourt bow maker known as
Grandadam, although she doesn't know its exact date. She uses a Jargar
E string, and her lower strings are Eudoxa Olives.*

been prepared to talk about that first, reluctant recording, and to reveal how ill prepared she felt for it.

Steve J. Sherman

"I was very worried about what doing a recording was like," she recalls. "When I asked André Previn, he said, 'Oh, just play as you did in the concerts. You know the pieces, so there'll be no problem.' I then had to admit to him that I'd never actually played the Sibelius with an orchestra before, and for a split second his face turned gray! He managed to recover very quickly and said everything would be fine. I could not have had a better person to record my first disc with. He is the most experienced studio musician, and a most sympathetic conductor."

The success of that disc in 1970 led to an exclusive contract with Decca, under which Chung was allowed to record whatever she liked—but this was usually much less than Decca wanted. From the earliest days of her relationship with the company, remembers Minshull, she was extremely self-critical.

At 22, Chung played the Tchaikovsky Concerto with the London Symphony Orchestra under the direction of André Previn.

In 1980 she took a complete break from performing. Aware that the pace of her career might easily cause her to compromise her artistic standards, Chung was used to subjecting herself to intense critical scrutiny. But one day she simply walked into her management's offices and declared she wanted to take a year off. She recalls that "they all fell off their chairs" but agreed to let her have six months to take stock. Although the period that followed was difficult, she found it invaluable. "I stopped going at full speed and slammed on the brakes. For a while I didn't know where I was, and I've never really recovered from that. But thank goodness I did it. I continued all the while to search and develop, and I was far more aware of how my playing was than I am now. I've never regretted it."

In the late '80s she moved from Decca to EMI (she switched, she says, because she wanted to work with different conductors) but by then she'd married and had two sons. Determined that her first commitment would be to her children, she drastically reduced her workload and slowed down the pace of her professional life. Only now that her sons are older does she feel able to refocus on her career and to increase the number of performances she gives.

Now a return to touring means that she can play her favorite works all around the world, exploring a relatively small repertoire in great depth. Her focus is currently on the Brahms concerto and sonatas. The sonatas form an interesting cycle, not least because the second and third are progressively less lyrical than the first. Does she think of them as individual works rather than a linked series of three? "Well, they work beautifully together, although as a composition the last sonata stands most impressively on its own. My favorite is really the first, the G-Major. To me it almost relates to his very late works." She asks me which one touches me the most.

The G-Major, I say, is for me the most obviously attractive and the most beautiful to listen to, but I agree that the D-Minor is the most impressive. "That's why a lot of young players start with the D-Minor," she explains. "It's an easier work for them to hold in front of the public. For me, the G-Major was very difficult. I was terrified when I first performed it. And that was in my early 30s; whereas, I've been playing the D-Minor since I was 16." She leans forward in her chair, grins broadly, and moves her hands energetically. "The A-Major is the happiest of all. Of the three, I'd say it's the weakest, but the last movement is just *divine*!

Columbia Artists

"But there's no weak Brahms composition. This man had a phenomenal gift. Bruch lived in his shadow, and he hated his own G-Minor Concerto because the public so identified him with it. You know, the other day I was listening to the radio in a taxi and heard a composition that was . . . well, all right. It turned out to be a concerto for two pianos by Bruch, and I thought: no wonder nobody plays it, when there's so much better work. Brahms' gift is *so* superior; the richness is an endless resource."

> To fully appreciate Chung's artistry, you have to watch her perform, not just listen to her.

Loving a work, however, doesn't make Chung enthusiastic to record it. If anything, she's more reluctant than ever to venture into the studio. Understandably, she says she wants to distance herself from the commercialism of much of the industry's activities, and she cites the soundtrack of the [1997] movie *Shine,* about the Australian concert pianist David Helfgott, as an example. To her, this isn't so much exploitation of a precarious talent as an inversion of the natural recorded order: success in the concert hall should have led to success in the cinema (and then on disc), not the other way around.

She says she is also suspicious of the industry's short-termism, and the way that some musicians are commodified according to fashion, their recordings disappearing from the catalog within months. She is not, she explains defiantly, that kind of artist. But why no recording of the Brahms Concerto, for instance, surely a staple of the repertoire?

"I've waited forever to do it, and now I almost wish I'd done it a long time ago so I could redo it. But one is changing constantly, and

whenever the release date for one of my recordings is announced, I wonder to myself whether I should have waited longer. The Brahms and the Beethoven concertos were the first things Decca wanted me to do, and they kept asking when they could expect them. I waited ten years before making my first recording of the Beethoven, and when they asked about the Brahms I kept saying, 'No, no; it's not possible.' It was only when I discovered [conductor] Carlos Kleiber that I wanted to do it, but of course that wasn't possible because he hardly ever works. So it just got pushed back. Now we're thinking of recording it in Vienna this year [1997] with Simon [Rattle]. And now that it finally might happen, I don't think I should be doing it! It's the most frightening prospect. I keep thinking: What for? How can I justify it?

Beneath the ice-cool exterior there is white-hot musical passion.

"But why is it at this point in my life, when music making seems more natural to me than ever, that I feel I have no ground to stand on? When I was younger my feet were planted absolutely firmly—I knew what I wanted to say and what I was going to say. And even if I wasn't so sure underneath, I had a certain amount of guts. Maybe I've simply become a gutless person! You don't need guts, though, just care and commitment to music making. Maybe that's the difference I feel. It's certainly still *wonderful* to make music."

I have listened carefully to this point, trying to understand why she's so wary of making records, especially when they're welcomed so eagerly. Is the reason simply that she's unwilling to commit a particular interpretation to disc when her opinions about a work are changing all the time? Surely the majority of musicians experience similar feelings?

"Some people consider making a recording as a kind of momentary document," she explains. "They just go in and do it. But for me it's such a soul-searching, personal confession. I have great doubts, and it involves a tremendous commitment and conviction. It's like opposites pulling, and it becomes more difficult as I get older. I can't help thinking: why do they need another recording? When I go to Japan, in particular, people scream at me, 'When is the next one coming out?' I reply that I don't want to be a liar, and that it comes out when it comes out."

Christopher Raeburn, who produced many of Chung's Decca recordings, says, "She's something of a perfectionist, so she'll never be totally satisfied. But I know she feels that certain discs do her justice." Chung herself admits that recordings do serve a purpose in educating the listener, especially since different interpretations resonate with different people. In her opinion, music communicates directly with the soul, regardless of the listener's previous knowledge, so a particular recording will be chosen and enjoyed because of its unique communicative capacity, while other versions won't be listened to for more than five minutes.

"I like to communicate to the public," she continues, "and after all these long years, I know I love performing in front of it. But because I'm physically not able to travel as much these days [a minor health complaint and the desire to spend more time with her family affected her at this period], I've certainly kept recording projects in mind. Recording is a way of reaching the public, but to me it must be in such a way that I can express something very personal. The content of the soul is very important."

Yet surely the consensus of critical opinion is that this is precisely what she achieves through her recordings? The 1970 Tchaikovsky/Sibelius coupling, for example, is still in the catalog and it remains, according to *Gramophone*'s reviewer, "a disc where both works are made to leap out at you in concentration and vitality." And what about her celebrated EMI recording of Bartók's Second Concerto with the City of Birmingham Symphony Orchestra under Simon Rattle?

"I probably shouldn't even try to express myself verbally about this. When I was younger I was very discontented and critical of myself, but I was still able to be more flexible and say, 'Well yes, I think it's good enough to release.' But now I really and truly can't tell. I really don't know. I mean, that Bartók recording received a *Gramophone* award, but I didn't want it to be released. I think it's dreadful. So I'm very hesitant to even talk about how I feel about my own work."

Does this suggest that she's becoming more self-critical as she gets older? "I *guess* that's being critical of oneself," she muses. "But the strange thing is that quite the opposite happens with live performances. When I was younger I used to run offstage, quite hysterical and totally discontented with what I'd done. I remember playing in a festival here in Nottingham in 1970 with the London Symphony Orchestra and Previn. I played the Sibelius Concerto and missed half a note in the cadenza. I cried all the way back to London; I thought I was finished. How could I make such a fool of myself in front of all those people? It was so important then that if

I missed one *tenth* of a note I thought it was the end of life. That attitude cannot continue unless you have total and unconditional discipline and you play in a vacuum, which of course isn't humanly possible. So I made a decision, and I acknowledged that technical perfection is not the end of music making. Technique has to be there, of course, and in a sense it's your duty, but its purpose is to serve the music. I therefore tried to find a balance.

"I like to communicate to the public, and...I love performing in front of it."

"She's a very unconventional violinist—by her own choice," says Raeburn. "It would be wrong to call her a maverick, but she makes her own agenda. That's very important." Analysis of Chung's repertoire throughout her career suggests that she hasn't exactly specialized in works outside the mainstream. She certainly has no desire to introduce lesser-known music on the basis that it's unfairly neglected, although one ambition that remains unfulfilled is to collaborate with a contemporary composer. She'd particularly like to explore the possibility of incorporating the idiom of Korean music into a new work, but the attempts so far have disappointed her. Her attitude toward such a project is essentially maternal, and she describes her hopes of "raising" a new work after helping it to be born. She nearly succeeded in the early '80s when working with the composer Andrej Tchaikowsky, but their collaboration was cut short when she gave birth to her son.

"He was working on an absolutely incredible piece, a gem, but it was never finished because the experience of becoming a mother meant that my career changed course. It couldn't have been otherwise. And although there are a lot of brilliant composers today who go about at a tremendous pace, that's not how I work. I'd like to collaborate with a composer and live with the work for the rest of my life, because it takes a long time for even a simple piece to go through my entire system. I had to work on Elgar's *Salut d'Amour* for two and a half years before I had the courage to play it in public, but now it's really part of me."

Unaccompanied Bach remains, for her, the ultimate in music making and thus the most daunting challenge of all, which is why she has not played it in public. But resuming her career has meant a welcome return to playing with chamber orchestras as soloist/director, which she began doing in the late '70s. "When I started again I suffered a dilemma, because while it's so satisfying to make music together directly—just making your own conversation—I felt I had to compromise certain musical points. At such moments you want a conductor to be there; on the other hand, when you're working with one you can't open your mouth. I always open mine, and that was always my problem.

"But sometimes people misinterpret your motives. When I did a chamber concert in Vienna with Sándor Végh [conductor and leader of the Végh Quartet], a young critic was terribly offended and complained that I dared to conduct in public with this great man. I had no intention of conducting the group; it was just my way of making music. Sándor Végh didn't move at all, but his presence was phenomenal—he created incredible textures with the slightest of movements. That was one of the greatest experiences in my learning process, and it will stay with me for the rest of my life. How little that critic understood!"

Chung's shyness is completely forgotten now. She launches into a conversation about her forthcoming concerts in London, and I am reminded once more that Kyung-Wha Chung is one of those individuals who could only ever have been a musician. She knows this, of course, and realizes how lucky she is. "Musicians are the most fortunate minority," she says. "If you truly love music and are committed to it, there isn't anything better in the world."

ABOUT THE CONTRIBUTORS

Edith Eisler is a violinist, violist, and teacher in New York, as well as a corresponding editor for *Strings* magazine. She began studying violin at the age of six in Vienna and later in Prague, with Max Rostal in London, and with Joseph Fuchs in New York. She performed solo and chamber music in Europe and North America and ran Music among Friends, a series of house concerts performed by New York–based professionals. She contributes to *Stagebill* and *Chamber Music* and reviews CDs and books for Amazon.com.

Robert Moon is a freelance classical-music journalist who wrote an internationally recognized book on early stereo London/Decca classical records, *Full Frequency Stereophonic Sound*. He holds a master's degree in arts administration from University of Wisconsin. He has served various arts organizations in administrative capacities, including the NEA, the Kansas Arts Commission, and the Minnesota Orchestra.

Andrew Palmer, a foreign correspondent for *Strings* magazine, lives in Nottingham, England, where he is a freelance writer and a photographer. His work has appeared on BBC Radio Three, as well as in *Gramophone, Soundscapes, The Flutist Quarterly,* and *Double Reed News*. He is the author of *Divas: In Their Own Words* and coauthor of *A Voice Reborn* (Arcadia Books, 1999).

Timothy Pfaff is the former editor of *Piano & Keyboard* magazine, music critic for the *San Francisco Examiner* and other U.S. newspapers and magazines, and West Coast correspondent for London's *Financial Times*. He currently lives in Laos, where he is writing music reviews for *Tipworld* and working on a book.

Russell Platt, a contributor to *Strings* magazine since 1995, is the lead classical-music reviewer of the *St. Paul Pioneer Press* and a noted composer. His reviews have appeared in *The New Yorker* and *Opera News,* and he has written program notes for the Boston Symphony Orchestra, the Minnesota Orchestra, and the Argo, Arabesque, Arsis, and Koch CD labels. His music has won awards from ASCAP and the American Academy of Arts and Letters and has been programmed by the Dale Warland Singers, the Saint Paul Chamber Orchestra, and the Aspen and Grand Teton Festivals, among others.

Julia Zaustinsky is a New York-based violinist, writer, and teacher. She has been a visiting artist and member of the faculty at major universities and conservatories in the United States and Europe and writes for Sony Classical, *Education Musicale,* and numerous journals. She has received awards for her work as a musician and writer from the National Society of Arts and Letters and the Committee on Pulitzer Prizes.

OTHER TITLES FROM STRING LETTER PUBLISHING

Musical Instrument Auction Price Guide, $44.95

Issued annually, illustrated with full-color plates of noteworthy instruments, the *Auction Price Guide* offers the most comprehensive information available on antique and handmade instrument and bow values. Asking and selling prices of instruments offered at the world's major auction houses are expressed in dollars, marks, pounds, and yen. A unique five-year summary by instrument and maker of high, low, and average prices shows market trends.

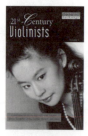

Commonsense Instrument Care Guide, $9.95

Violin maker and dealer James N. McKean, past president of the American Federation of Violin and Bow Makers, has written the essential reference on maintaining the playability and value of violins, violas, and cellos and their bows.

ALSO IN THE *STRINGS* BACKSTAGE SERIES

21st-Century Violinists, Vol. 1, $12.95

An exciting collection of in-depth interviews with the world's preeminent string players offer students, teachers, and music lovers insights into the fascinating lives of classical violin soloists. Whether they're child prodigies just entering the stage or cultural icons whose careers have had a lasting influence on generations of players, these series of conversations reveal how they practice, how they work with other musicians, their performance secrets and anxieties, what moves and inspires them, and much more.

21st-Century String Quartets, Vol. 1, $12.95

In this collection of in-depth interviews, today's leading performers get to the heart of one of the most beloved forms of classical music: the string quartet. You are backstage with the American, Borodin, Emerson, Guarneri, Juilliard, Mandelring, Manhattan, Mendelssohn, Orion, St. Petersburg, and Tokyo String Quartets. Members share their insights into the joys and hardships of expressing themselves as part of a tight-knit ensemble.

For more information on books from String Letter Publishing, or to place an order, please call Music Dispatch at (800) 637-2852 or fax (414) 774-3259, or mail to Music Dispatch, PO Box 13920, Milwaukee, WI 53213. Visit String Letter Publishing on-line at www.stringletter.com.